전 세계 1,600만이 입증한
통문장 학습법

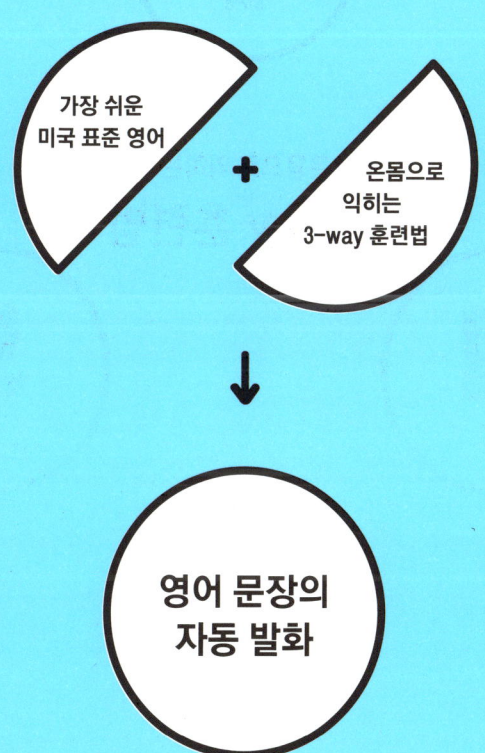

온몸으로 익히는
3-way 훈련법

무한 반복

ENGLISH 900

2

Edwin T. Cornelius, Jr. 저

YBM

ENGLISH 900 전면개정판 ②

발행인	허문호
발행처	YBM
편집	정윤영
디자인	장선숙
삽화	이용택
마케팅	고영노, 김한석, 김동진, 박찬경, 문근호

초판발행 2017년 4월 7일
10쇄발행 2025년 8월 20일

신고일자 1964년 3월 28일
신고번호 제 1964-000003호
주소 서울시 종로구 종로 104
전화 (02) 2000-0515 [구입 문의] / (02) 2000-0463 [내용 문의]
팩스 (02) 2285-1523
홈페이지 www.ybmbooks.com

ISBN 978-89-17-22713-0

English 900
Original edition © 1971 by Edwin Cornelius, Jr.

All rights reserved.
English-Korean 1st edition © 2012 by Joanne Cornelius and YBM
English-Korean 2nd edition © 2017 by Joanne Cornelius and YBM

All rights reserved. No part of this publication may be reproduced, stored in a retrieval system, or transmitted in any form, or by any means, (electronic, mechanical, photocopying, recording or otherwise) without the prior written permission of both of the copyright owner and the publisher of this book.

이 책의 저작권은 저자에게 있으며, 책의 제호 및 디자인에 대한 모든 권리는 출판사인 YBM에게 있습니다.
서면에 의한 저자와 출판사의 허락 없이 내용의 일부 혹은 전부를 인용 및 복제하거나 발췌하는 것을 금합니다.
낙장 및 파본은 교환해 드립니다.
구입철회는 구매처 규정에 따라 교환 및 환불처리 됩니다.

어린아이처럼 배워라
그리고 반복하라!

영어 배우기에는 왕도가 없습니다. 자기 하기 나름입니다. 영어를 해야겠다는 마음이 얼마나 절실한지에 따라, 본인이 실제로 얼마나 노력하느냐에 따라 성과는 다르게 나타납니다. 하루 아침에 영어를 배우는 비법은 없습니다. 끊임없이 듣고 말하는 것이 제일 중요합니다.

예전에 아프리카 콩고에서 재미있는 연구를 했습니다. 영어를 한마디도 못하던 콩고 인이 3개월만에 영어를 완벽히 구사하게 되었습니다. 말소리만 들으면 영락없이 영어 원어민이었지요. 요인은 무엇이었을까요. 바로 아프리카에 구전 전통이 있어서 가능했던 일입니다. 복잡하게 생각하지 않고, 무조건 말과 발음을 흉내내는 것이죠. 글로 읽거나 쓰며 익히는 게 아니라 듣고 따라하며 외우는 구전 전통이 말 익히기엔 최고라는 걸 여실히 보여준 거죠. 어린아이들이 언어를 익히는 것을 생각해보십시오. 어린아이처럼 배우십시오. 머뭇거리거나 실수를 두려워하면 영어를 배울 수 없습니다

듣고 말하기의 실천법으로 제가 추천하는 방법은 '반복'입니다. 공부하는 내용을 완전히 자기 것으로 만들기 위해서는 '반복'이 필수이지요. 그래서 저는 수년간 듣고 말하기의 반복을 구현한 학습 교재 개발에 힘썼고 English 900 시리즈가 바로 그 결과물입니다. 이 교재를 가지고 듣고 말하는 데 주력하십시오. 학교 시절 배운 문법이나 어휘, 문장들 모두 다 여러분의 머릿속 어딘가에 있습니다. 이 교재는 여러 분들이 이미 배웠던 내용들이 듣고 말하기, 반복의 방식을 통해 다시 입 밖으로 나오도록 매우 효과적으로 도와줍니다. 말과 발음에 더욱 집중할 수 있도록 헤드폰을 끼고 열심히 듣고 따라 하십시오.

제가 혼신의 힘을 기울여 개발한 이 English 900 시리즈가 여러분의 영어 공부에 큰 힘이 되어드릴 것을 자신합니다.

Edwin T. Cornelius, Jr.

글로벌 베스트셀러
English 900

1963년 초판

2013년 한국어 개정판

2014년 일본 개정판   2015년 중국어 개정판

언어학자 Cornelius가 미국 정부의 의뢰를 받아 만든 미국 표준 영어 교재

English 900은 전 세계에 미국 표준 영어를 보급하고자 미국 국무부가 미시간 대학에 의뢰하여 언어학자 Cornelius가 오랜 시간 연구하고 개발한 영어 교재입니다. 1970년대에는 대한민국 최초 오디오 교재로 출간되어 최다 판매를 기록하는 센세이션을 일으켰고, 전 세계적으로도 1,600만 부 이상 판매된 초대형 베스트셀러입니다.

English 900의 명성과 효과를 검증한 국내 개정판

English 900의 명성은 계속 그 대를 이어와 국내 독자들의 재출간 요청이 꾸준히 있었습니다. 2013년 드디어 대한민국 대표 영어 강사 이보영, 아이작 선생님의 친절하고 자세한 해설강의로 한층 업그레이드된 한국어 개정판 New English 900이 출간되었고, 2016년까지 총 22만 부가 판매되어 다시금 그 명성과 학습효과를 입증했습니다.

일본 열도와 중국 대륙까지 점령한 English 900 열풍

English 900의 재출간을 열망한 것은 대한민국의 학습자뿐만이 아니었습니다. 2014년 일본 아사히 프레스, 2015년 중국 금일금중 출판사도 개정판 출간의 대열에 합류하여 2,30대 젊은 영어 학습자들에게 좋은 반응을 얻고 있습니다.

2017년 한국어 전면개정판
무엇이 업그레이드되었나?

2017년 한국어 전면개정판

오리지널 English 900의 정통성과 장점은 그대로 살렸습니다! 1

희미한 옛 기억 속 중학교 영어 교과서에서 본 듯한 익숙한 문장들---일상생활에서 실제로 쓰이는 실용적이고 매우 쉬운 문장들만으로도 얼마든지 의사소통이 자유롭다는 Cornelius 박사의 믿음을 전면개정판에서도 그대로 이어가고 있습니다.

지금 세대의 일상 주제와 그들이 말하는 표준영어를 담았습니다! 2

전 세계의 문화는 급변했고 현 세대의 언어생활 또한 실용성을 추구하는 방향으로 변화하고 있습니다. 따라서 전면개정판에서는 교재의 문장과 대화문을 통해 다루고 있는 일상의 장면들 중 현 세대와 맞지 않는 일부 주제 및 문장들을 지금의 영어권 사람들이 말하는 영어로 교체했습니다.

통문장학습법의 실천법까지 제공해드립니다! 3

전면개정판에서는 '학습해야 할 것(what to learn)'뿐만 아니라 '학습하는 방법(how to learn)'을 함께 제시합니다. 통문장 두뇌입력 프로그램, 다양한 형식의 훈련용 MP3 파일이 통문장학습의 든든한 조력자가 될 것입니다.

English 900으로 이룬
5분의 작은 기적

2016년 여름 경북매일신문의 "전교생 48명, 포항 시골 장기초교 '5분의 작은 기적'"이라는 제목의 기사를 통해 New English 900 교재를 활용하여 영어공부를 하는 초등학생들과 교사들이 소개된 바 있습니다. English 900 온라인 카페의 성실멤버이기도 한 이 학교의 교장, 이성규 선생님을 만나보았습니다.

'5분의 작은 기적' 이란?

이성규 교장선생님 다른 행사 취재차 학교를 방문했던 기자가 우연히 우리 학교의 5분 영어 프로그램 설명을 듣고 감명을 받아 직접 교실을 방문하고 취재하여 '5분의 작은 기적'이라는 제목으로 신문에 소개한 것이죠. New English 900 초급 교재를 활용하여 제가 직접 개발한 컴퓨터 프로그램으로 매일 1교시 수업 전에 5분간 선생님들이 지도한 결과 학생들이 게임만 하던 컴퓨터로 영어 공부를 하고, 평가 프로그램으로 스스로 평가하고, 선생님께 상도 받으면서 즐겁게 공부를 하게 되었습니다.

English 900을 교재로 택하신 이유는?

이성규 교장선생님 English 900은 학생 시절 다 마스터하지 못했다가 2013년에 새롭게 출시된 New English 900으로 다시 공부를 시작한 것이지요. 900개 기본 문장을 지금 11번째 복습 중인데, 이 교재의 좋은 점은 900이라는 뚜렷한 목표점을 가지고 공부할 수 있다는 것이지요. 학교에서 사용하는 영어 교과서도 좋지만 세계적으로 검증된 교재를 가지고 아이들이 초급회화 300문장이라는 목표에 우선적으로 도전하게 하면, 졸업 후까지도 계속 연결하여 공부할 수 있겠다는 생각으로 이 교재를 선택했습니다.

이성규 교장선생님 1권에 수록되어 있는 초급회화 300문장은 교과서에 나오는 문장도 많이 있어서 고학년에서는 300문장을 모두 마스터한 아이도 있습니다. 1학년부터 6학년까지 전교생이 100개까지는 거의 마스터했으니 계속 지도한다면 가능하다고 생각됩니다. 교사가 직접 모든 내용을 가르치기보다는 학생들이 스스로 공부할 수 있는 마인드를 키워주니 무리 없이 잘 따라오고 있습니다.

어른들 교재인데 아이들에게 어렵지 않았나?

이성규 교장선생님 English 900은 말하기 위주의 학습에 더 효과적이라고 생각합니다. 저도 듣기는 약하지만 이제 말하기는 어느 정도 자신이 있습니다. 이 책의 900개 기본 문장은 우리말만 봐도 거의 0.5초 내에 영어 문장이 나옵니다. 물론 900 문장만 외운다고 해서 말하기가 완벽히 된다고 할 수는 없지만 다른 표현까지 응용하여 말할 수 있는 기본 실력을 갖추게 된다고 생각합니다.

900개 통문장이 정말 효과가 있었나?

이성규 교장선생님 학습한 횟수도 중요하지만 내가 학습한 내용을 얼마나 알고 있는지 확인해보는 것이 중요하다고 생각합니다. 종이에 쓰면서 확인해도 좋지만, 우리의 궁극적인 목표가 '말하기'이니 영어로 직접 말해보고 음원으로 바로 정답을 확인하면 더욱 효과적일 것 같아서 개발한 프로그램이 '자율평가 프로그램'입니다. 학습한 내용을 스스로 평가하여 확인하면 더욱 동기 부여가 되겠지요. 또 정기적으로 원어민과 대화할 수 있는 기회를 마련하여 학습한 내용을 활용하는 것도 중요합니다.

다른 학습자들에게 전수하고픈 노하우는?

English 900으로
이런 효과 보았다!

영어회화 학습자의 마지막 선택

저도 영어회화에 한(?)이 맺혀서 정말 수많은 방법론에 매달려 많은 시간을 보냈어요. 그러다가 찾아낸 보물 같은 영어회화 교재가 English 900이었죠. 이 책의 최대 강점은 영어회화의 목표와 분량이 확실하다는 것입니다. 제가 공부한 경험으로는 900개의 문장은 아주 적당한 분량이며 수준도 어렵지 않아요. 이 교재로 반복해서 우리말을 듣고 영어로 말하는 훈련을 하다 보면, 하고 싶은 우리말이 떠오르는 순간 영어가 입에서 자동으로 튀어나오는 놀라운 경험을 하게 될 것입니다.

31만 방문 블로그 '영어백편의자현' 운영자, 김동건

영어 말하기 연습을 위한 최고의 교재

English 900은 제가 대학을 다닐 때 선풍적인 인기를 끌었던 영어회화 교재였어요. 아마 지금 40대 이상의 부모님들에게는 매우 친숙한 이름이 아닐까 싶습니다. 영어교사를 준비하던 저는 900개의 기본 문장들과 거기에서 파생된 문장들을 외워가며 English 900과 씨름을 했어요. 책이 점점 낡아가는 정도와 비례해 영어회화에 대한 자신감은 커져갔고, 간혹 만나는 외국인들 앞에서 하고 싶은 말들이 튀어나올 때 그 신기함과 희열은 이루 말할 수가 없었습니다.

차준식 영어교실 운영자, 고등학교 영어교사, 차준식

저 보고 English 900 전도사래요

2년 전 이 책을 만나 그 효과를 실감한 저는 그 후 1년간 주변의 많은 사람들에게 이 책을 권하지 않을 수 없었죠. 저에게 소개 받은 분들이 또 다른 분들에게 추천하는 식으로 그렇게 김해의 많은 분들이 이 책을 공부하게 되었어요. 도서관에서 이 책에 관심을 보이는 사람들끼리 스터디 모임도 결성해 주 1회 함께 공부도 했는데, 작년에는 이 책으로 저와 함께 1년간 공부한 50대 지인의 영어 실력이 눈에 띄게 향상되고 자신 있게 해외 자유여행도 다녀오셨다고 하여 보람을 느꼈답니다. 새로 개정되는 책도 영어를 공부하는 많은 이들에게 등불 같은 존재가 되길 기원해봅니다.

초등학교 방과후 영어강사, 장은주

영어회화 학습의 정석이네요

직장인이 되어 사무 현장에서 영어 쓸 일을 직접 겪다 보니, 영어를 잘하고 싶다는 마음이 학교 다닐 때보다 더 간절하게 듭니다. 영어 잘하는 직장 선배에게 조언을 구하니 무조건 말하고 외우는 게 정석이라고 하네요. New English 900에 반영된 코넬리우스의 영어회화 학습법이 딱 맞을 것 같더군요. 공부해보니 역시나 이만한 학습법은 없는 것 같습니다. 반복해서 말하고 트레이닝하다 보니 어느새 표현이 입에 착착 붙네요.

28세, 직장인, 이희원

강사도 추천하는 교재입니다

English 900에는 실생활에서 쓰이는 어렵지 않은 영어 문장 900개가 들어 있어, 혼자서도 쉽게 공부할 수 있는 교재입니다. 예전부터 이 교재에 대해 알고 있어서, 주변에서 쉬운 영어 교재를 추천해달라고 할 때마다 주저 없이 권했습니다.

35세, 영어강사, 최지웅

부담 없어요

900개 문장만 공부하면 영어가 된다고 해서 이게 무슨 말인가 했어요. 한편으로는 900개면 너무 많은 거 아닌가 생각도 했었는데, 막상 책을 보고 하루에 하라는 만큼만 하니 부담스럽지 않던데요. 혼자 영어 공부하기 부담되시는 분들에게 적절한 교재 같아요.

23세, 대학생, 원미향

쉬운 단어로 이루어진 문장이 좋아요

직장을 관두고 영어와는 담을 쌓고 지내왔는데 영어를 더 멀리하면 안 되겠다는 생각에 English 900을 공부했습니다. 책에서 제시하는 대로 계속 반복해서 듣고 말하니 나중에는 진짜 영어 문장을 보지 않아도 입에서 문장이 나오네요. 어려운 단어를 사용하지 않아도 영어로 말할 수 있다는 걸 이번에 처음 알았습니다.

32세, 전업주부, 황미경

English 900 사용설명서

4단계 학습으로
기본 문장 300개 반복 훈련

STEP 1 통문장 말하기

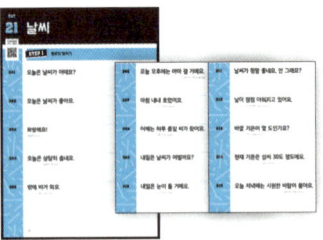

기본 문장을 5개씩 먼저 우리말로 보고 영어로 말해보세요. 말이 되든 안 되든 직접 말해보세요.

STEP 2 통문장 외우기

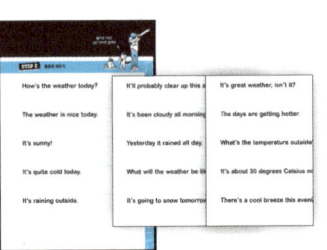

왼쪽 페이지에서 우리말을 보고 스스로 말해본 것을 이제 확인하며 암기하세요. 큰 소리로 2회 읽으세요.

STEP 3 패턴으로 훈련하기

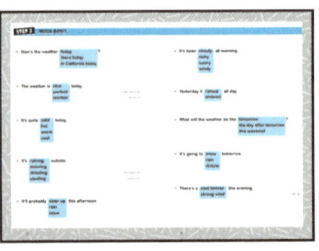

패턴 형태로 앞에서 배운 기본 문장을 한번 더 반복하여 암기 효과뿐 아니라 응용할 수 있는 역량까지 기르세요.

STEP 4 대화로 훈련하기

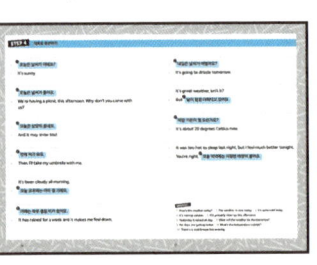

의사소통의 핵심은 대화죠. 대화의 기본 형태인 묻고 답하기 방식으로 기본 문장의 쓰임을 익히세요.

다양한 MP3 파일로 300문장 귀에 새기기!

통문장 말하기
우리말 문장 듣기 → 스스로 영어로 말해보기 → 영어 문장 듣고 확인하기

통문장 외우기
우리말 문장 듣기 → 영어 문장 2회 따라 말하기

패턴으로 훈련하기
영어 문장 1회 따라 말하기

대화로 훈련하기
영어 문장 1회 따라 말하기

통문장 영어만 듣기
출퇴근길, 소리 내어 훈련할 수 없을 때 기본 문장만 영어로 빠르게 듣기

총 5가지 종류의 MP3 파일을 활용하여
300문장의 암기 효과를 높여보세요!

통문장 두뇌입력 프로그램으로
300문장 뇌에 새기기!

통문장 두뇌입력 프로그램 이란?

2단계 구성을 통해 통문장을 눈으로 보고, 귀로 듣고, 입으로 말하며 반복 훈련하는 트레이닝용 동영상이에요.

1단계 청크 단위 암기 훈련

> STEP 1
> 청크 단위 암기 훈련
> "문장을 덩어리씩 늘려가며 큰소리로 따라 말해봅시다!"

처음부터 문장 전체를 외우는 게 부담스럽다면 문장을 덩어리씩 늘려가며 훈련하면 단기간에 통문장 학습에 적응할 수 있어요.

2단계 자동 발화 훈련

> STEP 2
> 자동 발화 훈련
> "우리말 문장을 영어로 말해본 후, 들려주는 영어 문장을 2회 따라 합시다!"

1단계에서 누적 학습한 효과로 통문장이 입에서 자동으로 나오는 것을 확인하며 말하기에 대한 자신감을 얻는 단계예요.

이런 좋은 프로그램을 어디서 만날 수 있죠?

각 Day의 첫 페이지에 있는 QR 코드를 휴대폰으로 찍으면 바로 재생하여 편리하게 학습할 수 있어요.

두뇌입력 프로그램 활용을 위한
QR 코드 이용법

1 STEP
QR 코드가 있는
각 Day 시작 페이지를
펼쳐보세요.

2 STEP
네이버 어플리케이션을
실행하여 QR 코드를
읽어 보세요.

검색창 옆에 마이크 모양을 누르세요.

여러 아이콘들 중 QR 코드 모양을
누르세요.

카메라 화면이 나오면 교재의
QR 코드를 읽을 수 있게 가까
이 대주세요.

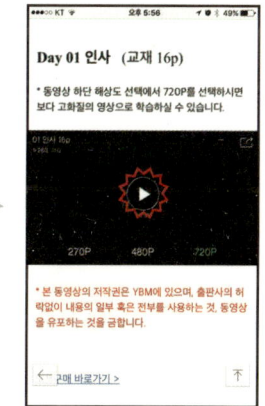

QR 코드가 제대로 읽히면 두뇌입력
프로그램으로 바로 연결됩니다. 세모
모양의 버튼을 누르면 재생됩니다.

* 네이버 어플리케이션 외에
도 QR 코드를 읽어주는 여
러 어플리케이션이 있습니
다. 구글 플레이스토어 또는
아이폰 앱스토어에서 "QR코
드 리더"로 검색하셔서 관련
어플리케이션을 설치해 사용
하셔도 됩니다.

English 900 ❷ 목차

일상회화 통문장 300개

Day 21	날씨	16
Day 22	사물 묘사	26
Day 23	부탁과 요청	36
Day 24	길 찾기	46
Day 25	전화	56
Day 26	스마트폰과 SNS	66
Day 27	결혼과 가정	76
Day 28	거주지와 이웃	86
Day 29	내일 일과	96
Day 30	의복 관리	106

Day 31	매장 쇼핑	116
Day 32	온라인 쇼핑	126
Day 33	음식 주문	136
Day 34	영화 및 공연 관람	146
Day 35	예약	156
Day 36	진료	166
Day 37	집 구하기	176
Day 38	계획	186
Day 39	이동 수단	196
Day 40	여행 준비	206

ENGLISH 900 ①
기초회화 통문장
300개

ENGLISH 900 ③
프리토킹 통문장
300개

21 날씨

STEP 1 통문장 말하기

301 오늘은 날씨가 어때요?

302 오늘은 날씨가 좋아요.

303 화창해요!
화창한 sunny

304 오늘은 상당히 춥네요.
상당히, 꽤 quite

305 밖에 비가 와요.
비가 오다 rain

STEP 2 통문장 외우기

How's the weather today?

The weather is nice today.

It's sunny!

It's quite cold today.

It's raining outside.

STEP 1 　 통문장 말하기

306 　 오늘 오후에는 아마 갤 거예요.
　　　　　　　　　　(날씨가) 개다 clear up

307 　 아침 내내 흐렸어요.
　　　　　　　　흐린 cloudy

308 　 어제는 하루 종일 비가 왔어요.
　　　　　　　　　　하루 종일 all day

309 　 내일은 날씨가 어떨까요?

310 　 내일은 눈이 올 거예요.
　　　　　　　　　눈이 오다 snow

STEP 2 통문장 외우기

It'll probably clear up this afternoon.

It's been cloudy all morning.

Yesterday it rained all day.

What will the weather be like tomorrow?

It's going to snow tomorrow.

STEP 1　통문장 말하기

311　날씨가 정말 좋네요, 안 그래요?

312　날이 점점 더워지고 있어요.
　　　　더 더워지다 get hotter

313　바깥 기온이 몇 도인가요?
　　　　기온 temperature

314　현재 기온은 섭씨 30도 정도예요.
　　　　섭씨 Celsius

315　오늘 저녁에는 시원한 바람이 불어요.
　　　　산들바람, 미풍 breeze

STEP 2 통문장 외우기

It's great weather, isn't it?

The days are getting hotter.

What's the temperature outside?

It's about 30 degrees Celsius now.

There's a cool breeze this evening.

STEP 3 패턴으로 훈련하기

❶ How's the weather today ?
there today
in California today

❷ The weather is nice today.
perfect*
terrible*

*완벽한, 더할 나위 없는
*매우 좋지 않은

❸ It's quite cold today.
hot
warm
cool

❹ It's raining outside.
snowing
drizzling*
sleeting*

*(비가) 보슬보슬 내리다
*진눈깨비가 내리다

❺ It'll probably clear up this afternoon.
rain
snow

❻ It's been [cloudy / rainy / sunny / windy] all morning.

❼ Yesterday it [rained / snowed] all day.

❽ What will the weather be like [tomorrow / the day after tomorrow / this weekend]?

❾ It's going to [snow / rain / drizzle] tomorrow.

❿ There's a [cool breeze / strong wind*] this evening.

*강한 바람

STEP 4 대화로 훈련하기

A ① 오늘은 날씨가 어때요?

B It's sunny.

A ② 오늘은 날씨가 좋아요.

B We're having a picnic this afternoon. Why don't you come with us?

A ③ 오늘은 상당히 춥네요.

B And it may snow too!

A ④ 밖에 비가 와요.

B Then I'll take my umbrella with me.

A It's been cloudy all morning.

B ⑤ 오늘 오후에는 아마 갤 거예요.

A ⑥ 어제는 하루 종일 비가 왔어요.

B It has rained for a week and it makes me feel down.

A ❼ 내일은 날씨가 어떨까요?

B It's going to drizzle tomorrow.

A It's great weather, isn't it?

B But ❽ 날이 점점 더워지고 있어요.

A ❾ 바깥 기온이 몇 도인가요?

B It's about 25 degrees Celsius now.

A It was too hot to sleep last night, but I feel much better tonight.

B You're right. ❿ 오늘 저녁에는 시원한 바람이 불어요.

ANSWERS!!

1 How's the weather today?   2 The weather is nice today.   3 It's quite cold today.
4 It's raining outside.   5 It'll probably clear up this afternoon.
6 Yesterday it rained all day.   7 What will the weather be like tomorrow?
8 the days are getting hotter.   9 What's the temperature outside?
10 There's a cool breeze this evening.

22 사물 묘사

STEP 1 통문장 말하기

316 당신의 휴대폰은 무슨 색이에요?

317 연한 파란색이에요.
(강도가) 약한 light

318 어떤 크기의 노트북을 갖고 있어요?
노트북 laptop (computer)

319 제 노트북들 중 하나는 작고, 다른 하나는 중간 크기예요.
(크기 등이) 중간의 medium

320 그 데스크톱의 랜 케이블 길이가 얼마나 돼요?
데스크톱, 탁상용 컴퓨터 desktop (computer)   랜 케이블, 랜 선 LAN cable

STEP 2 통문장 외우기

What color is your cell phone?

It's light blue.

What size laptop do you have?

One of my laptops is small, and the other one is medium size.

How long is the LAN cable for the desktop?

STEP 1 통문장 말하기

321 길이가 겨우 5미터예요.
겨우 only

322 저 여행 가방은 무게가 얼마나 나가요?
여행 가방 suitcase   무게가 ~이다 weigh

323 5파운드 정도 나가요.

324 너무 무거운 건 아닌데 정확한 무게는 모르겠어요.
정확한 exact

325 이 창문이 저 창문보다 더 넓어요?
더 넓은 wider

STEP 2 통문장 외우기

It is only 5 meters long.

How much does that suitcase weigh?

It weighs about 5 pounds.

It's not too heavy, but I don't know the exact weight.

Is this window wider than that one?

STEP 1 통문장 말하기

326 아니오, 이 창문은 딱 저 창문만큼 넓어요.
~만큼 넓은 as wide as

327 저 테이블의 모양이 마음에 들어요.
모양, 형태 shape

328 저는 정사각형인 것보다 둥근 것이 더 좋아요.
정사각형의 square   B보다 A를 선호하다 prefer A to B

329 그 옷의 촉감이 어때요?
(촉감이) ~하다 feel

330 아주 부드러워요.

STEP 2 통문장 외우기

No, this window is just as wide as that one.

I like the shape of that table.

I prefer the round one to the square one.

How does the cloth feel?

It feels very soft.

STEP 3   패턴으로 훈련하기

① What color is your cell phone ?
   new sweater
   backpack*

*등에 메는 배낭형 가방

② It's light blue .
   dark* green
   bright* red

*(색상이) 짙은

*(색상이) 밝은

③ What size laptop do you have?
   refrigerator*
   monitor*

*냉장고

*(컴퓨터) 화면, 모니터

④ One of my laptops is small , and the other one is medium size.
   large
   big

⑤ How much does that suitcase weigh?
   box
   package*

*소포

❻ It's not too heavy , but I don't know the exact weight.
        very light*
        fairly heavy   *가벼운

❼ This window is just as wide   as that one.
                          narrow*   *(폭이) 좁은
                          high and wide

❽ I like the shape of that table.
              size
              color

❾ I prefer the round one to the square one.
                long   short*   *짧은
                big   little*   *작은

❿ It feels very soft .
                 hard*   *단단한
                 sticky*   *끈적거리는

STEP 4　대화로 훈련하기

A　❶ 당신의 휴대폰은 무슨 색이에요?
B　It's bright red.

A　Is your new sofa yellow?
B　No, ❷ 연한 파란색이에요.　Yellow is not my favorite color.

A　What size laptop do you have?
B　❸ 제 노트북들 중 하나는 작고, 다른 하나는 중간 크기예요.

A　❹ 그 데스크톱의 랜 케이블 길이가 얼마나 돼요?
B　It is only 3 meters long.

A　❺ 저 여행 가방은 무게가 얼마나 나가요?
B　I guess it weighs about 5 pounds.

A　How much does that package weigh?
B　❻ 너무 무거운 것까진 아닌데 정확한 무게는 모르겠어요.

A **❼이 창문이 저 창문보다 더 넓어요?**

B No, this window is just as narrow as that one.

A **❽저 테이블의 모양이 마음에 들어요.**

B It doesn't match our other furniture.

A Would you like a square button for that shirt?

B No, **❾저는 정사각형인 것보다 둥근 것이 더 좋아요.**

A **❿그 옷의 촉감이 어때요?**

B It feels very soft and smooth.

ANSWERS!!

1 What color is your cell phone?   2 it's light blue.
3 One of my laptops is small, and the other one is medium size.
4 How long is the LAN cable for the desktop?
5 How much does that suitcase weigh?
6 It's not too heavy, but I don't know the exact weight.
7 Is this window wider than that one?   8 I like the shape of that table.
9 I prefer the round one to the square one.   10 How does the cloth feel?

DAY 23 부탁과 요청

STEP 1 통문장 말하기

331 집안일에 당신 도움이 필요해요.
집안일 chores

332 빨래 좀 도와줄 수 있어요?
빨래, 세탁물 laundry   ~할 수 있다 be able to

333 도와줘서 고마워요.

334 천만에요.

335 집안일을 거들어줄래요?
집안일, 가사 housework

STEP 2 통문장 외우기

I need your help with the chores.

Are you able to help me with the laundry?

Thank you for your help.

You're welcome.

Can you help with the housework?

STEP 1   통문장 말하기

336 저 쓰레기를 내다 버려주시겠어요?
쓰레기 trash   내다 버리다 take out

337 제 부탁 좀 들어줄래요?
~의 부탁을 들어주다 do ~ a favor

338 존에게 불을 켜 달라고 해주세요.
(전기 등을) 켜다 turn on

339 시간이 있으면 내일 전화 좀 줄래요?

340 이 무거운 상자를 들어 올리는 것 좀 도와주시겠어요?
들어 올리다 lift

STEP 2 통문장 외우기

Would you please take out the trash?

Will you do me a favor?

Please ask John to turn on the lights.

If you have time, will you call me tomorrow?

Would you help me lift this heavy box?

STEP 1   통문장 말하기

341   피터슨 씨에게 제가 여기 있다고 전해주시겠어요?

342   저 대신 고양이에게 먹이를 주시면 안 될까요?
                   먹이를 주다 feed   언짢아하다 mind

343   물론이죠. 먹이를 얼마나 줘야 하죠?
         (동의, 받아들임의 뜻으로) 천만에요, 물론이에요 not at all

344   드라이버를 이쪽으로 건네주시겠어요?
               ~으로 건네주다 pass over

345   후추를 다 썼으면 제게 주시겠어요?
            다 끝난, 완료된 done

STEP 2 통문장 외우기

Would you please tell Mr. Peterson that I'm here?

Would you mind feeding my cat for me?

Not at all. How much should I feed him?

Could you pass the screwdriver over here?

Could I have the pepper when you're done with it?

STEP 3 패턴으로 훈련하기

❶ I need your help with the chores / something / this document*

*서류, 문서

❷ Are you able to help me with the laundry / this project* / my homework* ?

*프로젝트, 과제
*숙제

❸ Thank you for your help / kindness* / support*.

*친절
*지지, 지원

❹ Would / Will / Could you please take out the trash?

❺ Please ask John to turn on the lights / turn the lights on / turn off* the lights / turn the lights off.

*(전기 등을) 끄다

42

❻ **If you have time**, will you call me tomorrow?
If you're able to
If you think of* it

*~이 생각나다

❼ Would you help me **lift** this heavy box?
carry*
move*

*나르다
*옮기다

❽ Would you please **tell Mr. Peterson** that I'm here?
let Mr. Peterson know
remind* Mr. Peterson

*상기시키다, 알려주다

❾ Would you mind **feeding my cat** for me?
mailing* this package
calling* Mr. Smith

*우편으로 보내다
*전화를 걸다

❿ **Could you pass** the screwdriver over here?
Would you pass
Would you mind passing

STEP 4   대화로 훈련하기

A ① 집안일에 당신 도움이 필요해요.
B Oh, I hate housework!

A Thank you for your kindness.
B ② 천만에요.   I'm glad I could help.

A ③ 저 쓰레기를 내다 버려주시겠어요?
B Let me just finish writing this e-mail.

A ④ 제 부탁 좀 들어줄래요?
B Sure, what is it?

A It's so dark in here, isn't it?
B ⑤ 존에게 불을 켜 달라고 해주세요.

A ⑥ 시간이 있으면 내일 전화 좀 줄래요?
B Sure, what time is best for you?

A ❼ 피터슨 씨에게 제가 여기 있다고 전해주시겠어요?

B I'm sorry but he's just stepped out.

A ❽ 저 대신 고양이에게 먹이를 주시면 안 될까요?

B Not at all. Where is the cat food?

A Hey, I'm ready to do anything to help you.

B ❾ 드라이버를 이쪽으로 건네주시겠어요?

A ❿ 후추를 다 썼으면 제게 주시겠어요?

B Sure, go ahead.

ANSWERS!!

1 I need your help with the chores. 2 You're welcome.
3 Would you please take out the trash? 4 Will you do me a favor?
5 Please ask John to turn on the lights. 6 If you have time, will you call me tomorrow?
7 Would you please tell Mr. Peterson that I'm here?
8 Would you mind feeding my cat for me? 9 Could you pass the screwdriver over here?
10 Could I have the pepper when you're done with it?

24 길 찾기

STEP 1 통문장 말하기

346 실례하지만 힐튼 호텔을 찾는 것 좀 도와줄래요?

347 곧장 앞으로 두 블록만 가면 됩니다.
곧장 straight 앞으로 ahead

348 피스 공원까지 가는 길을 알려주시겠어요?
길을 알려주다 give directions

349 다음 모퉁이에서 오른쪽으로 도세요.
모퉁이 corner   (방향을) 돌다 turn

350 피치로(路)가 어디 있는지 알려주시겠어요?

STEP 2 통문장 외우기

Excuse me, can you help me find the Hilton Hotel?

It's 2 blocks straight ahead.

Can you give me directions to the Peace Park?

Turn right at the next corner.

Can you tell me where Peach Street is?

STEP 1 통문장 말하기

351 이 길로 가야 하나요, 아니면 저 길로 가야 하나요?

352 모르겠어요. 저도 여기 초행이에요.
처음 온 사람 stranger

353 영화관은 어느 방향인가요?
영화관 movie theater

354 모퉁이를 돌면 바로 있어요.
모퉁이를 돈 곳에 around the corner

355 워싱턴 대학교까지 얼마나 먼지 아세요?

STEP 2 통문장 외우기

Should I go this way, or that way?

I don't know. I'm a stranger here, too.

Which way is the movie theater?

It's just around the corner.

Do you know how far it is to Washington University?

STEP 1 통문장 말하기

356 여기서부터 한참 가야 돼요.

357 저쪽 길로 두 블록 간 다음 왼쪽으로 도세요.

358 가장 가까운 지하철역이 어디 있는지 알려주시겠어요?
가장 가까운 the nearest

359 플라자 호텔에서 길 건너편에 있어요.
건너편에, 맞은편에 across

360 쉽게 찾을 수 있어요.
(못 보고) 놓치다 miss

STEP 2 통문장 외우기

It's a long way from here.

Go that way for 2 blocks, then turn left.

Could you tell me where the nearest subway station is?

It's across the street from the Plaza Hotel.

You can't miss it.

STEP 3 패턴으로 훈련하기

❶ Excuse me, can you help me find the Hilton Hotel / the Imperial Theater / an ATM* ?

*현금자동입출금기

❷ Turn right / Go to the left / Go straight ahead at the next corner.

❸ Can you tell me where Peach Street / the restroom / the restaurant is?

❹ I don't know. I'm a stranger here, too / not from around here / not familiar with* the area .

*~에 익숙한, 잘 아는

❺ It's just around the corner / right on the corner / in the middle* of the block / up there on the left . You can't miss it.

*가운데, 중간

6. Do you know how far it is to Washington University ?
   where the train station is
   the way to* the bank   *~으로 가는 길

7. It's a long way from here.
   short distance*   *거리
   short walk*   *도보
   long drive*   *운전

8. Go that way for 2 blocks , then turn left.
   a block or 2
   about 200 meters

9. Could you tell me where the nearest subway station is?
   hospital*   *병원
   bank*   *은행

10. It's across the street from the Plaza Hotel.
    around the corner
    50 meters straight ahead

STEP 4 대화로 훈련하기

A ① 실례하지만 힐튼 호텔을 찾는 것 좀 도와줄래요?
B Turn right at the next corner.

A Excuse me, can you help me find an ATM?
B ② 곧장 앞으로 두 블록만 가면 됩니다.

A ③ 피스 공원까지 가는 길을 알려주시겠어요?
B Of course. Go to the left at the next corner.

A Can you tell me where Peach Street is?
④ 이 길로 가야 하나요, 아니면 저 길로 가야 하나요?
B Go this way then you can find it.

A Can you tell me where the Grant Hotel is?
B ⑤ 모르겠어요. 저도 여기 초행이에요.

A ⑥ 영화관은 어느 방향인가요?
B It's right on the corner.

A 워싱턴 대학교까지 얼마나 먼지 아세요?

B It's a short distance from here.

A Do you know where the train station is?

B 저쪽 길로 두 블록 간 다음 왼쪽으로 도세요.

A 가장 가까운 지하철역이 어디 있는지 알려주시겠어요?

B It's 50 meters straight ahead from the Plaza Hotel.

A Can you tell me how to get to the bank?

B It's across the street from the subway station. 쉽게 찾을 수 있어요.

ANSWERS!!

1 Excuse me, can you help me find the Hilton Hotel?   2 It's 2 blocks straight ahead.
3 Can you give me directions to the Peace Park?   4 Should I go this way, or that way?
5 I don't know. I'm a stranger here, too.   6 Which way is the movie theater?
7 Do you know how far it is to Washington University?
8 Go that way for 2 blocks, then turn left.
9 Could you tell me where the nearest subway station is?   10 You can't miss it.

DAY 25 전화

STEP 1 통문장 말하기

361 전화가 울려요. 좀 받아주시겠어요?
전화를 받다 answer

362 여보세요, 마이크로칩 사의 재닛입니다.
주식회사 Inc.[incorporated]

363 여보세요, 매기와 통화할 수 있을까요?

364 (당신은) 전화 잘못 걸었어요.
전화를 걸다 dial

365 더 크게 말해주시겠어요?

STEP 2 통문장 외우기

The phone is ringing. Can you answer it, please?

Hello, Microchips Inc. This is Janet speaking.

Hello, may I speak to Maggie?

You must have dialed the wrong number.

Could you please speak louder?

STEP 1 통문장 말하기

366 잠깐만 기다려주세요.
(수화기를 들고) 기다리다 hold

367 어떤 사람이 당신을 (전화상으로) 기다리고 있어요.
전화상에 있는 on the line

368 전화 거신 분이 누군지 물어봐도 될까요?

369 미안해요. 그녀는 전화를 받을 수 없어요.
만날 수 있는, 바쁘지 않은 available

370 메모를 남기시겠어요?
남기다 leave

STEP 2 통문장 외우기

Please hold for a minute.

Someone is on the line for you.

May I ask who is calling?

I'm sorry. She's not available.

Would you like to leave a message?

STEP 1   통문장 말하기

371 그녀에게 제가 전화했다고 전해주시겠어요?

372 내일 언제 다시 전화하시면 안 될까요?
다시 전화하다 call back

373 쿠퍼 씨에게 전화하려고 했는데 계속 통화 중이었어요.
통화 중이다 the line is busy

374 맞는 번호로 걸었는데 아무도 받지 않았어요.

375 그의 휴대폰으로 연락하면 돼요.
(전화로) 연락하다 reach

STEP 2 통문장 외우기

Would you please tell her that I called?

Would you mind calling back sometime tomorrow?

I tried to call Mr. Cooper, but the line was busy.

I dialed the right number, but nobody answered.

You can reach him on his cell phone.

STEP 3　패턴으로 훈련하기

❶ The phone is ringing.　**Can you answer it**, please?
　　　　　　　　　　　　Will you get it for me
　　　　　　　　　　　　Would you pick it up*　　　　*들어올리다
　　　　　　　　　　　　Would you see who's calling

❷ **Hello, Microchips Inc.**　This is James speaking.
　 Hello, you've reached YBM.
　 Marketing*.　　　　　　　　　　　　*마케팅(부)

❸ Hello, **may I speak to Maggie** ?
　　　　　 is Maggie there

❹ **You must have dialed** the wrong number.
　 You must have
　 I think you've got

❺ I'm sorry. **She's not available**.
　　　　　　 She can't come to the phone right now
　　　　　　 She's on another* **call**　　　　*또 다른

❻ Would you like to leave | a message | ?
| your name |
| your name and number |

❼ Would you please tell her that | I called | ?
| I'll call her later |
| I'll call her back tomorrow |

❽ Would you mind | calling back | sometime tomorrow?
| calling again |
| returning* his call |

*~에 답하다

❾ I tried to call Mr. Cooper, but | the line was busy | .
| nobody answered |
| his phone was disconnected* |

*연결을 끊다

❿ You can reach him | on his cell phone | .
| at this number |
| on Facebook |

63

STEP 4 대화로 훈련하기

A **① 전화가 울려요. 좀 받아주시겠어요?**
B I'm sorry, I can't. I'm doing the dishes.

A **② 여보세요, 마이크로칩 사의 재닛입니다.**
B Hello, may I speak to Ms. Marilyn Peters?

A Hello, is Maggie there?
B **③ (당신은) 전화 잘못 걸었어요.**

A Can you hear me now?
B Sorry. **④ 더 크게 말해주시겠어요?**

A Hello, may I speak to Nancy?
B **⑤ 잠깐만 기다려주세요.**

A **⑥ 전화 거신 분이 누군지 물어봐도 될까요?**
B This is Claire from YBM.

A Good afternoon. May I please speak to your manager?

B ❼ 미안해요. 그녀는 전화를 받을 수 없어요.

A ❽ 메모를 남기시겠어요?

B Would you please tell her that I'll call her later?

A I've got to go. Let's talk some other time.

B Sure. ❾ 내일 언제 다시 전화하시면 안 될까요?

A I tried to call Mr. Cooper, but the line was busy.

B ❿ 그의 휴대폰으로 연락하면 돼요.

ANSWERS!!

1 The phone is ringing. Can you answer it, please?
2 Hello, Microchips Inc. This is Janet speaking.
3 You must have dialed the wrong number.   4 Could you please speak louder?
5 Please hold for a minute.   6 May I ask who is calling?   7 I'm sorry. She's not available.
8 Would you like to leave a message?
9 Would you mind calling back sometime tomorrow?
10 You can reach him on his cell phone.

DAY 26 스마트폰과 SNS

STEP 1 통문장 말하기

376 인터넷 접속이 안 돼요.
(인터넷에) 접속하다 access

377 와이파이 비밀번호를 입력해야 해요.

378 주소록에 제 번호를 저장해 놔요.

379 집에 도착하면 문자를 보낼게요.
문자를 보내다 send a text

380 휴대폰을 떨어뜨렸더니 액정에 금이 갔어요.
금이 간, 갈라진 cracked

STEP 2 통문장 외우기

I can't access the Internet.

You need to enter a Wi-Fi password.

Put my number in your address book.

I'll send you a text when I get home.

I dropped my cell phone and the screen is cracked.

STEP 1   통문장 말하기

381   배터리 충전이 안 돼요.
충전하다 charge

382   전화기를 수리점으로 보내세요.
수리점 repair center

383   왜 전화를 안 받았어요?

384   미안해요. 전화기를 무음 모드로 설정해 놓았거든요.
무음의 silent

385   제 전화기의 메모리가 사진과 동영상 때문에 꽉 찼어요.
가득 찬, 빈 공간이 없는 full

STEP 2 통문장 외우기

The battery won't charge.

Send your phone to the repair center.

Why didn't you answer the phone?

I'm sorry. I set my phone to silent mode.

The memory on my phone is full because of photos and videos.

STEP 1 통문장 말하기

386 공간이 확보되도록 파일들을 좀 지우세요.
공간을 내다 make space

387 저는 휴대폰으로 블로그를 해요.
블로그를 기록하다 blog

388 상사가 페이스북에서 친구 신청을 했어요.
(SNS 등에) 친구 신청을 하다 friend

389 이제 그가 상태를 업데이트할 때마다 '좋아요'를 눌러야겠네요.
상태, 상황 status

390 그가 트위터에서도 당신을 팔로우하고 있던데요.
또한 as well

STEP 2 통문장 외우기

Delete some of the files to make space.

I blog from my phone.

My boss friended me on Facebook.

Now, you should "like" his every status update.

He's following you on Twitter as well.

STEP 3 패턴으로 훈련하기

❶ I can't access the Internet .
my e-mail account
your Web site

❷ You need to enter a Wi-Fi password .
your e-mail address
your banking information*

*금융 정보

❸ Put   my number in your address book .
Add*   to your contacts
Delete*   from your phone

*추가하다
*삭제하다

❹ I'll send you a text when I get home .
when I'm ready
as soon as* I can

*~하자마자

❺ I dropped my cell phone and the screen is cracked .
the screen turned* black
it won't turn on

*~이 되다

❻ Why didn't you [answer the phone / text me back / set an alarm* on your phone]?   *자명종을 맞추다

❼ I set my phone to [silent / vibrate* / sound] mode.   *진동

❽ Delete [some of the files / old messages and photos / useless applications*] to make space.   *애플리케이션, 앱

❾ I [blog / send emails / post on Facebook] from my phone.

❿ [My boss friended me / A friend of mine has blocked* me / More than* 100 people "liked" my post] on Facebook.   *막다, 차단하다   *~보다 많이, ~이상(의)

73

STEP 4   대화로 훈련하기

A ① 인터넷 접속이 안 돼요.
B   You need to enter a Wi-Fi password.

A   Put my number in your address book.
B ② 집에 도착하면 문자를 보낼게요.

A ③ 휴대폰을 떨어뜨렸더니 액정에 금이 갔어요.
B   Send your phone to the repair center.

A   What's wrong with your phone?
B ④ 배터리 충전이 안 돼요.

A ⑤ 왜 전화를 안 받았어요?
B   I left it in my bag, so I couldn't hear the phone ringing.

A   Do you know how many times I called you last night?
B ⑥ 미안해요. 전화기를 무음 모드로 설정해 놓았거든요.

A The memory on my phone is full because of photos and videos.
B ❼ 공간이 확보되도록 파일들을 좀 지우세요.

A ❽ 저는 휴대폰으로 블로그를 해요.
B Let me link to your blog. What's the URL?

A You look so worried.
B ❾ 상사가 페이스북에서 친구 신청을 했어요.

A He subscribes to my blog.
B ❿ 그가 트위터에서도 당신을 팔로우하고 있던데요.

ANSWERS!!

1 I can't access the Internet.   2 I'll send you a text when I get home.
3 I dropped my cell phone and the screen is cracked.   4 The battery won't charge.
5 Why didn't you answer the phone?   6 I'm sorry. I set my phone to silent mode.
7 Delete some of the files to make space.   8 I blog from my phone.
9 My boss friended me on Facebook.   10 He's following you on Twitter as well.

DAY 27 결혼과 가정

STEP 1 통문장 말하기

391 우리 결혼해요!
결혼하다 get married

392 그 사람이 저와 결혼하자고 했어요.
결혼하다 marry

393 결혼식에 와주셨으면 좋겠어요.
(시간 안에) 도착하다 make

394 결혼한 지 얼마나 됐나요?

395 이제 막 결혼했어요.
막 just

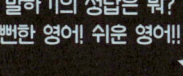

STEP 2 통문장 외우기

We're getting married!

He asked me to marry him.

I hope you can make the wedding.

How long have you been married?

We've just married.

STEP 1   통문장 말하기

396   우리는 신혼여행 중이에요.
~의 신혼여행 중인 on one's honeymoon

397   우리는 결혼한 지 몇 년 됐어요.
꽤 많은, 상당한 수의 quite a few

398   우리는 2007년에 결혼했어요.

399   남동생은 결혼했나요?

400   결혼하지 않았어요. 아직 미혼이에요.
아직, 여전히 still

STEP 2 통문장 외우기

We're on our honeymoon.

We've been married for quite a few years.

We got married in 2007.

Is your brother married?

He's not married. He's still single.

STEP 1   통문장 말하기

401 그는 1년 넘게 이혼한 상태예요.
이혼한 divorced

402 자녀들이 있나요?

403 곧 아빠가 될 거예요.

404 우리는 지난달에 아기를 낳았어요.
아기를 낳다 have a baby

405 우리 아이들은 이제 다 컸어요.
다 큰, 장성한 grown up

STEP 2 통문장 외우기

He's been divorced for over a year.

Do you have children?

I'm going to be a father.

We had a baby last month.

Our children are grown up now.

STEP 3 패턴으로 훈련하기

① He asked me to **marry him** .
   be his wife
   go out with* him   *~와 사귀다

② I hope you can make the **wedding** .
   party tonight
   meeting next week

③ How long have you been **married** ?
   dating*   *~와 데이트를 하다
   separated*   *별거 중인

④ We've been married **for quite a few years** .
   for nearly* 3 years   *거의
   since* last April   *~이래로

⑤ **We** got married in 2007.
   My niece*   *조카딸
   His nephew*   *조카 (아들)

❻ Is your | brother / daughter / cousin* | married?

*사촌

❼ Do you have | children / any children / a child | ?

❽ I'm going to be a | father / grandfather | .

❾ We had | a baby / a child / another child | last month.

❿ Our children | are grown up / are married / have children of their own | now.

STEP 4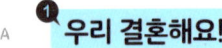

A **① 우리 결혼해요!**

B Congratulations!

A **② 그 사람이 저와 결혼하자고 했어요.**

B That's good news. I'm so happy for you.

A **③ 결혼식에 와주셨으면 좋겠어요.**

B Of course! We'd be honored.

A **④ 결혼한 지 얼마나 됐나요?**

B We've just married. We're on our honeymoon.

A When did you get married?

B **⑤ 우리는 2007년에 결혼했어요.**

A Is your brother married?

B **⑥ 결혼하지 않았어요. 아직 미혼이에요.**

A Is your cousin still single?
B Well, ❼ 그는 1년 넘게 이혼한 상태예요.

A ❽ 자녀들이 있나요?
B Not yet, but I'm ready to have children.

A ❾ 곧 아빠가 될 거예요.
B I'm so excited for you! When is the baby due?

A How old are your children?
B ❿ 우리 아이들은 이제 다 컸어요.

ANSWERS!!
1 We're getting married!   2 He asked me to marry him.
3 I hope you can make the wedding.   4 How long have you been married?
5 We got married in 2007.   6 He's not married. He's still single.
7 he's been divorced for over a year.   8 Do you have children?
9 I'm going to be a father.   10 Our children are grown up now.

28 거주지와 이웃

STEP 1 통문장 말하기

406 바로 이 동네에서 자랐나요?
동네 neighborhood

407 저는 캘리포니아에서 어린 시절을 보냈어요.
(시간을) 보내다 spend

408 10살이 될 때까지 캘리포니아에서 살았어요.
~까지 until

409 그러고 나서 우리 가족은 이곳으로 이사 왔어요.
이사 오다 move in

410 이곳은 제가 17살까지 자란 곳이에요.

STEP 2 통문장 외우기

Did you grow up right here in this neighborhood?

I spent my childhood in California.

I lived in California until I was 10.

Then my family moved in here.

This is where I grew up until I was 17.

STEP 1 통문장 말하기

411 지난 20년간 여기에서 많은 변화들이 있었어요.
지난 last

412 저 모퉁이에 식료품 가게가 있었어요.
식료품 가게 grocery store   (과거 한때에는) ~이었다, 했다 used to

413 저 집들은 모두 지난 10년 사이에 지어졌어요.

414 저는 이 동네의 모든 것들이 정말 좋아요.

415 이 지역에선 모든 것이 매우 편리해요.
지역 area   편리한 convenient

STEP 2 통문장 외우기

There have been a lot of changes here in the last 20 years.

There used to be a grocery store on the corner.

All of those houses have been built in the last 10 years.

I love everything in this neighborhood.

Everything is so convenient in this area.

STEP 1 통문장 말하기

416 이웃들은 친절한가요?
친절한 friendly

417 우리 모두 서로를 꽤 잘 알아요.
서로 each other   어느 정도, 꽤 pretty

418 옆집엔 누가 살아요?
옆집 next door

419 젊은 부부가 우리 옆집으로 이사 왔어요.
젊은 부부 a young married couple

420 저는 그들과 잘 지내요.
잘 지내다 get along well

STEP 2 통문장 외우기

Are your neighbors friendly?

We all know each other pretty well.

Who lives next door?

A young married couple moved in next door to us.

I get along well with them.

STEP 3 패턴으로 훈련하기

① Did you grow up right here in this neighborhood / city / little town ?

② I spent my childhood / early childhood / early years* in California. *어린 시절

③ I lived in California / Seoul / Japan until I was 10.

④ This is where I grew up until I was / my wife grew up until she was / the twin* brothers grew up until they were 17. *쌍둥이

⑤ There have been a lot of changes / developments* / improvements* here in the last 20 years. *발달 *개선

❻ There used to be a | grocery store | on the corner.
　　　　　　　　　　　 | pharmacy* |
　　　　　　　　　　　 | movie theater |

*약국

❼ | All | of those houses have been built in the last 10 years.
　 | Some |
　 | Many |
　 | Almost* all |

*거의

❽ Are your neighbors | friendly | ?
　　　　　　　　　　 | kind |
　　　　　　　　　　 | quiet* |
　　　　　　　　　　 | noisy* |

*조용한
*시끄러운

❾ | We all | know each other pretty well.
　 | Some of us |
　 | Most* of us |

*대부분

❿ A young married couple | moved in | next door to us.
　　　　　　　　　　　　 | is going to move in |

93

STEP 4 대화로 훈련하기

A Did you grow up right here in this neighborhood?
B ① 저는 캘리포니아에서 어린 시절을 보냈어요.

A When did you leave California?
B ② 10살이 될 때까지 캘리포니아에서 살았어요.

A Then where did you move to?
B ③ 그러고 나서 우리 가족은 이곳으로 이사 왔어요.

A ④ 이곳은 제가 17살까지 자란 곳이에요.
B You must have lots of childhood memories here.

A ⑤ 지난 20년간 여기에서 많은 변화들이 있었어요.
B Fortunately, the house where I was born is still here.

A Look at the huge shopping center!
B ⑥ 저 모퉁이에 식료품 가게가 있었어요.

A The houses here are very modern.
B ❼ 저 집들은 모두 지난 10년 사이에 지어졌어요.

A I love everything in this neighborhood.
B So do I. ❽ 이 지역에선 모든 것이 매우 편리해요.

A Are your neighbors friendly?
B ❾ 우리 모두 서로를 꽤 잘 알아요.

A ❿ 옆집엔 누가 살아요?
B A young married couple moved in next door to us.

ANSWERS!!

1 I spent my childhood in California.   2 I lived in California until I was 10.
3 Then my family moved in here.   4 This is where I grew up until I was 17.
5 There have been a lot of changes here in the last 20 years.
6 There used to be a grocery store on the corner.
7 All of those houses have been built in the last 10 years.
8 Everything is so convenient in this area.   9 We all know each other pretty well.
10 Who lives next door?

DAY 29 내일 일과

STEP 1 통문장 말하기

421　내일 몇 시에 일어날 거예요?

422　아마 6시 30분에 일어날 거예요.

423　그런 다음 뭘 할 거예요?
　　　그 다음에, 그러고는 then

424　옷을 입은 후 아침 식사를 할 거예요.
　　　옷을 입다 get dressed

425　내일 아침 식사로 뭘 먹을 거예요?
　　　　　　아침 식사로 for breakfast

목표는 단 하나.
1초의 주저함도 없이
자동으로 튀어나오게 하라!

STEP 2 통문장 외우기

What time are you going to get up tomorrow?

I'll probably get up at 6:30.

What will you do then?

After I get dressed, I'll have breakfast.

What will you have for breakfast tomorrow?

STEP 1 통문장 말하기

426 아침 식사로 달걀과 토스트를 먹을 것 같아요.

427 아침 식사 후에 출근 준비를 할 거예요.
~할 준비를 하다 get ready to

428 8시에 집을 나서서 사무실에는 8시 30분에 도착할 거예요.
떠나다 leave

429 저는 아마 12시 30분쯤에 점심 식사하러 나갈 거예요.
~하러 나가다 go out for

430 저는 6시에 일을 마치고 8시까지는 집에 도착할 거예요.
~까지 by

STEP 2 통문장 외우기

I guess I'll have eggs and toast for breakfast.

After breakfast, I'll get ready to go to work.

I'll leave the house at 8 o'clock and get to the office at 8:30.

I'll probably go out for lunch at about 12:30.

I'll finish working at 6 and get home by 8 o'clock.

STEP 1 통문장 말하기

431 내일 밤 집에서 저녁 식사할 거예요?

432 내일 아침에 영화를 보러 갈 생각인가요?

433 집에 있으면서 TV를 볼 것 같은데요.
집에 머물다 stay home

434 졸리면 아마 자러 갈 거예요.
졸리다 get sleepy

435 내일 아침에 일찍 일어날 수 있을 것 같아요?

STEP 2   통문장 외우기

Are you going to have dinner at home tomorrow night?

Do you think you'll go to the movies tomorrow morning?

I think I'll stay home and watch TV.

When I get sleepy, I'll probably get ready for bed.

Do you think you'll be able to get up early tomorrow morning?

STEP 3 패턴으로 훈련하기

❶ What time | are you / are we / is she | going to get up tomorrow?

❷ | I'll / We'll / She'll | probably get up at 6:30.

❸ What will you do | then / after that / next | ?

❹ What | will you / are you going to / do you think you'll | have for breakfast tomorrow?

❺ After breakfast, I'll get ready to | go to work / leave* the house / walk* my dog |.

*떠나다
*~와 산책하다

❻ I'll finish | working / typing* this report / reviewing* all documents | at 5:30.

*타자하다, 입력하다
*검토하다

❼ Are you going to | have dinner at home / cook for your family / have a birthday party | tomorrow night?

❽ Do you think | you'll / he'll / Peter and John will | go to the movies tomorrow morning?

❾ When I get sleepy, I'll probably | get ready for bed / drink some coffee / turn off the lights | .

❿ Do you think | you'll / the baby will / they'll | be able to get up early tomorrow morning?

STEP 4 대화로 훈련하기

A **① 내일 몇 시에 일어날 거예요?**

B I'll probably get up at noon. I'm off work tomorrow.

A What will you do then?

B **② 옷을 입은 후 아침 식사를 할 거예요.**

A **③ 내일 아침 식사로 뭘 먹을 거예요?**

B I won't have anything for breakfast. I'm on a diet.

A **④ 아침 식사로 달걀과 토스트를 먹을 것 같아요.**

B Then don't forget to buy some eggs on the way home!

A Are you ready to leave?

B **⑤ 아침 식사 후에 출근 준비를 할 거예요.**

A **⑥ 8시에 집을 나서서 사무실에는 8시 30분에 도착할 거예요.**

B I'm afraid you'll be late for work.

A What time are you going to have lunch?
B ❼ 저는 아마 12시 30분쯤에 점심 식사하러 나갈 거예요.

A Are you going to have dinner at home tomorrow night?
B I guess so. ❽ 저는 6시에 일을 마치고 8시까지는 집에 도착할 거예요.

A ❾ 내일 아침에 영화를 보러 갈 생각인가요?
B I'll probably stay home and watch TV.

A How late are you going to be awake?
B ❿ 졸리면 아마 자러 갈 거예요.

ANSWERS!!

1 What time are you going to get up tomorrow?
2 After I get dressed, I'll have breakfast.
3 What will you have for breakfast tomorrow?
4 I guess I'll have eggs and toast for breakfast.
5 After breakfast, I'll get ready to go to work.
6 I'll leave the house at 8 o'clock and get to the office at 8:30.
7 I'll probably go out for lunch at about 12:30.
8 I'll finish working at 6 and get home by 8 o'clock.
9 Do you think you'll go to the movies tomorrow morning?
10 When I get sleepy, I'll probably get ready for bed.

30 의복 관리

STEP 1 통문장 말하기

436 이제 옷을 입지 않겠어요? 그러다 버스를 놓치겠어요.
~하지 않겠니? why don't you~?   (짐작으로) ~지도 모른다 might

437 두꺼운 재킷을 입는 게 좋을 거예요. 오늘은 쌀쌀해요.
~하는 게 더 낫다 would better   쌀쌀한 chilly

438 오늘 뭘 입을 거예요?

439 검은색 정장을 입을 거예요.
정장 suit

440 그 정장을 세탁하고 다림질해야 해요.
~를 세탁하고 다림질하다 have ~ cleaned and pressed

STEP 2 통문장 외우기

Why don't you get dressed now?
You might miss the bus.

You'd better wear a heavy jacket.
It's chilly today.

What are you going to wear today?

I'm going to wear my black suit.

You need to have that suit cleaned and pressed.

STEP 1 통문장 말하기

441 제 정장이 모두 더러워요. 입을 게 없어요.
더러운, 지저분한 dirty

442 드라이클리닝을 해야 하는 정장이 두 벌 있어요.
드라이클리닝한 dry-cleaned

443 세탁소에 가져갈 셔츠들이 좀 있어요.

444 이 셔츠들을 세탁하고 다림질해야 해요.
~를 세탁하고 다림질하다 get ~ washed and ironed

445 이 드레스는 더 이상 제게 맞지 않네요.
(의복 등이) 맞다 fit

STEP 2 통문장 외우기

All my suits are dirty. I don't have anything to wear.

I have 2 suits that need to be dry-cleaned.

I have some shirts to take to the cleaners.

I've got to get these shirts washed and ironed.

This dress doesn't fit me anymore.

STEP 1　통문장 말하기

446　이 단추를 못 채우겠어요.
채우다, 매다 fasten

447　제가 너무 자라서 어떤 옷들은 안 맞아요.
너무 커져 맞지 않게 되다 outgrow

448　이 구두들은 닳았어요.
닳은 worn out

449　새 옷을 입고 있는 걸 미처 몰랐어요.
알아채다, 눈치채다 notice

450　저는 들어와서 옷을 갈아입고 다시 나갔어요.
갈아입다 change

STEP 2 통문장 외우기

I can't fasten this button.

I've outgrown some of my clothes.

These shoes are worn out.

I didn't notice you were wearing your new clothes.

I came in, changed my clothes, and went out again.

STEP 3 패턴으로 훈련하기

❶ You'd better wear | a heavy jacket | . It's | chilly | today.
| a light jacket | | warm |
| gloves | | freezing* |

*꽁꽁 얼게 추운

❷ What are you going to wear | today | ?
| tomorrow |
| on your date* |

*(남녀간의) 데이트

❸ I'm going to wear | my black suit | .
| a skirt and a blouse |
| jeans and a T-shirt |

❹ You need to have that suit | cleaned and pressed | .
| dry-cleaned |
| ironed |

❺ All my suits are | dirty | . I don't have anything to wear.
| wrinkled* |
| out of date* |

*주름이 있는
*유행이 지난

❻ I have | 2 suits | that I need to take to the cleaners.
         | a coat |

❼ I have | some shirts | to take to the cleaners.
         | dresses and scarves* |
         | some dirty clothes |

*스카프(scarf)의 복수형

❽ I've got to get | these shirts | washed and ironed.
                 | this dress |
                 | these sheets |

❾ | This dress doesn't | fit me anymore.
  | These pants don't |
  | These shoes don't |

❿ I didn't notice you were wearing | your new clothes | .
                                   | a new hat |
                                   | a ring* |

*반지

STEP 4 대화로 훈련하기

A: I need your help. I spent hours choosing what to wear today!
B: ① 이제 옷을 입지 않겠어요? 그러다 버스를 놓치겠어요.

A: ② 두꺼운 재킷을 입는 게 좋을 거예요. 오늘은 쌀쌀해요.
B: But the heavy jacket doesn't go with this skirt at all.

A: ③ 오늘 뭘 입을 거예요?
B: I'm going to wear my black suit.

A: Oops! I just spilled coffee on my suit.
B: ④ 그 정장을 세탁하고 다림질해야 해요.

A: ⑤ 제 정장이 모두 더러워요. 입을 게 없어요.
B: You can wear your sister's suit, if she'd like.

A: Where are you headed?
B: ⑥ 세탁소에 가져갈 셔츠들이 좀 있어요.

A **❼ 이 셔츠들을 세탁하고 다림질해야 해요.**

B You can pick them up tomorrow.

A **❽ 이 드레스는 더 이상 제게 맞지 않네요.**

B Tell me about it. I've outgrown some of my clothes too.

A Why are you throwing all your shoes away?

B **❾ 이 구두들은 닳았어요.** I can't wear them.

A **❿ 새 옷을 입고 있는 걸 미처 몰랐어요.**

B How do I look?

ANSWERS!!

1 Why don't you get dressed now? You might miss the bus.
2 You'd better wear a heavy jacket. It's chilly today.
3 What are you going to wear today?   4 You need to have that suit cleaned and pressed.
5 All my suits are dirty. I don't have anything to wear.
6 I have some shirts to take to the cleaners.
7 I've got to get these shirts washed and ironed.   8 This dress doesn't fit me anymore.
9 These shoes are worn out.   10 I didn't notice you were wearing your new clothes.

31 매장 쇼핑

STEP 1 통문장 말하기

451 옷을 좀 사야 해서 쇼핑하러 가요.

452 뭘 도와 드릴까요?

453 그냥 둘러보는 거예요.
　　　둘러보다 look around

454 이 드레스는 실크로 만들어진 거죠, 그렇지 않나요?
　　　~으로 만든 made of

455 이 스웨터를 입어 보고 싶어요.
　　　입어 보다 try on

STEP 2　통문장 외우기

I'm going shopping because I need to buy some clothes.

Can I help you with anything?

I'm just looking around.

This dress is made of silk, isn't it?

I'd like to try on this sweater.

STEP 1 통문장 말하기

456 어떤 사이즈로 드릴까요?

457 이 옷의 중간 치수가 필요해요.

458 참 잘 어울리네요.
~와 잘 어울리다 look good on

459 정말 좋아요! 두 벌 살게요.
선택하다, 사다 take

460 이 셔츠는 얼마죠?

STEP 2 통문장 외우기

What size would you like?

I need this in a medium.

That looks very good on you.

I love it! I'll take two.

How much is this shirt?

STEP 1 통문장 말하기

461 이 의자는 오늘 세일하나요?
　　　　　　　　할인[세일] 중인 on sale

462 좋은 태블릿 피시네요. 근데 너무 비싸요.
　　　　　　　　　　　　　(값, 비용이) 들다 cost

463 이게 작동되지 않으면 나중에 다시 가져와도 되나요?
　　　　작동되다 work

464 이건 어떻게 지불하시겠어요?
　　　　　　　~을 지불하다 pay for

465 신용카드는 받나요?
　　　　　　받다 take

STEP 2 통문장 외우기

Is this chair on sale today?

That's a nice tablet PC, but it costs too much.

If this doesn't work, may I bring it back later?

How would you like to pay for this?

Do you take credit cards?

STEP 3 패턴으로 훈련하기

❶ I'm going shopping because I need to buy some clothes / groceries* / gifts .

*식료품

❷ This dress is made of silk / wool / cotton* , isn't it?

*면

❸ I'd like to try on this sweater / this pair of shoes / these pants .

❹ I need this in a medium / size 7 / dark brown .

❺ That looks very good / just right* / too big / too small on you.

*딱 알맞은

❻ How much is | this shirt | ?
　　　　　　　| this coat |
　　　　　　　| that suit |

❼ Is this chair | on sale | today?　　　　　　　*50% 할인의
　　　　　　　| half off* |
　　　　　　　| 30 percent off |

❽ That's a nice tablet PC, but | it costs too much | .
　　　　　　　　　　　　　　　| it's too expensive |
　　　　　　　　　　　　　　　| I can't afford* to pay that much |
　　　　　　　　　　　　　　　　　　　　　　　　　　*(~을 살) 형편이 되다

❾ If this doesn't work, may I | bring it back | later?
　　　　　　　　　　　　　　　| exchange* it |　　*교환하다
　　　　　　　　　　　　　　　| return it |
　　　　　　　　　　　　　　　| get a refund* |　　*환불하다

❿ Do you take | credit cards | ?
　　　　　　　| Visa* |　　*비자 (신용카드)
　　　　　　　| traveler's checks* |　　*여행자 수표
　　　　　　　| US dollars |

STEP 4 대화로 훈련하기

A　❶ 옷을 좀 사야 해서 쇼핑하러 가요.
B　Why don't you wait until the sales start?

A　Can I help you with anything?
B　Thank you, but ❷ 그냥 둘러보는 거예요.

A　❸ 이 드레스는 실크로 만들어진 거죠, 그렇지 않나요?
B　Let me check it for you, ma'am.

A　❹ 이 스웨터를 입어 보고 싶어요.
B　The fitting rooms are to your left.

A　What size would you like?
B　❺ 이 옷의 중간 치수가 필요해요.

A　That looks very good on you.
B　❻ 정말 좋아요! 두 벌 살게요.

A **❼ 이 셔츠는 얼마죠?**

B It costs 50 dollars.

A **❽ 이 의자는 오늘 세일하나요?**

B I'm sorry, sir. We don't offer any discounts today.

A So what do you think of the tablet PC?

B **❾ 좋은 태블릿 피시네요. 근데 너무 비싸요.**

A How would you like to pay for this?

B **❿ 신용카드는 받나요?** I don't have any cash on me.

ANSWERS!!

1 I'm going shopping because I need to buy some clothes.   2 I'm just looking around.
3 This dress is made of silk, isn't it?   4 I'd like to try on this sweater.
5 I need this in a medium.   6 I love it! I'll take two.   7 How much is this shirt?
8 Is this chair on sale today?   9 That's a nice tablet PC, but it costs too much.
10 Do you take credit cards?

32 온라인 쇼핑

STEP 1 통문장 말하기

466 이거 아마존에서 샀어요.

467 어떤 결제 방식이 가능한가요?
받아주다 accept

468 신용카드나 페이팔로만 지불할 수 있어요.
~으로 지불하다 pay by

469 백화점에서 사는 것보다 저렴한가요?
값이 더 싼[저렴한] cheaper

470 물론이죠, 이 가방은 오늘의 특가로 샀는걸요.
특가 special price

STEP 2 통문장 외우기

I bought this on Amazon.

What forms of payment do they accept?

You can only pay by credit card or PayPal.

Is it cheaper than buying at the department store?

Of course, I got this bag at today's special price.

STEP 1　통문장 말하기

471 만약 제가 제품에 만족하지 못하면 어쩌죠?
~에 만족한 satisfied with

472 30일 환불 보장 제도가 있어요.
보장 guarantee

473 한국으로 배송하나요?
배송하다 ship

474 서울까지 물건을 배달 받으려면 얼마나 들어요?
~을 배달 받다 get ~ delievered

475 배송료는 주문한 물건의 크기와 무게에 따라 결정될 거예요
배송료 shipping charge　　　　　　　　　　　　　~에 따라 결정되다 depend on

STEP 2 통문장 외우기

What if I'm not satisfied with the product?

They have 30 day money-back guarantee.

Do they ship to Korea?

How much is it to get items delivered to Seoul?

The shipping charge will depend on the size and weight of your order.

STEP 1 통문장 말하기

476 도착하는 데 얼마나 걸릴까요?

477 주문한 다음 날에 배송 받을 수 있나요?
다음 날에 overnight

478 아니오, 최소한 4-5일은 걸릴 것 같아요.
최소한, 적어도 at least

479 배송 상황을 온라인으로 확인할 수 있나요?
추적하다 track

480 배송 주소를 변경할 수 있나요?

STEP 2 통문장 외우기

How long will it take to arrive?

Can it be shipped overnight?

No, I think it'll take 4 to 5 days at least.

Can I track the shipment online?

Can I change the delivery address?

STEP 3 패턴으로 훈련하기

❶ I bought this   on Amazon.
　　　　　　　　 on a social commerce* site
　　　　　　　　 online

*소셜커머스

❷ You can only pay by   credit card or PayPal.
　　　　　　　　　　　 cash
　　　　　　　　　　　 bank transfer*

*은행 송금

❸ Is it   cheaper   than buying at the department store?
　　　　 more expensive
　　　　 more comfortable*

*편안한

❹ I got this bag at   today's special   price.
　　　　　　　　　　 a lower*
　　　　　　　　　　 a reduced*

*더 낮은
*할인된

❺ What if   I'm not satisfied with the product   ?
　　　　　 there are any defects* with the product
　　　　　 they fail to ship my order on time*

*결함
*제때에

❻ Do they ship to Korea ?
　　　　　　　　internationally*　　　　　　　　　* 해외로
　　　　　　　　on Sundays

❼ How much is it to get items delivered to Seoul?
　　　　　　does it cost
　　　　　　do they charge

❽ The shipping charge will depend on
　　　　　　the size and weight of your order .
　　　　　　the shipping method*　　　　　　　* 방법, 수단
　　　　　　the distance to the destination*　　* 도착지

❾ Can it be shipped overnight ?
　　　　　　　　　　within* a week　　　　　　* ~이내에
　　　　　　　　　　by Wednesday

❿ I think it'll take 4 to 5 days at least .
　　　　　　　　　　3 working days
　　　　　　　　　　less than* 72 hours　　　　* ~보다 적은

STEP 4 대화로 훈련하기

A Where did you get that Bluetooth speaker?
B ① 이거 아마존에서 샀어요.

A ② 어떤 결제 방식이 가능한가요?
B You can only pay by credit card or PayPal.

A Is it cheaper than buying at the department store?
B ③ 물론이죠, 이 가방은 오늘의 특가로 샀는걸요.

A ④ 만약 제가 제품에 만족하지 못하면 어쩌죠?
B They have 30 day money-back guarantee.

A ⑤ 한국으로 배송하나요?
B I'm not sure if they have international shipping services on that website.

A How much is it to get items delivered to Seoul?
B ⑥ 배송료는 주문한 물건의 크기와 무게에 따라 결정될 거예요.

A **❼ 도착하는 데 얼마나 걸릴까요?**

B It will take at least 7 working days.

A **❽ 주문한 다음 날에 배송 받을 수 있나요?**

B No, I think it'll take 4 to 5 days at least.

A **❾ 배송 상황을 온라인으로 확인할 수 있나요?**

B Yes, we will send you the tracking number after we ship out your item.

A **❿ 배송 주소를 변경할 수 있나요?**

B Once your order has been submitted, you are unable to change the delivery address.

ANSWERS!!

1 I bought this on Amazon.   2 What forms of payment do they accept?
3 Of course, I got this bag at today's special price.
4 What if I'm not satisfied with the product?   5 Do they ship to Korea?
6 The shipping charge will depend on the size and weight of your order.
7 How long will it take to arrive?   8 Can it be shipped overnight?
9 Can I track the shipment online?   10 Can I change the delivery address?

33 음식 주문

STEP 1 통문장 말하기

481 주문하시겠어요?
주문을 받다 take an order

482 어떤 종류의 애피타이저가 있나요?
애피타이저, 식욕을 돋우기 위한 전채요리 appetizer

483 속을 채운 버섯, 토마토 샐러드, 그리고 그릴에 구운 양파가 있습니다.
채워 넣은 stuffed

484 스테이크와 생선 요리 중에 어느 것을 드시겠어요?
~하고 싶다 would rather

485 뉴욕 등심 스테이크로 주세요.
등심 sirloin

STEP 2　통문장 외우기

May I take your order?

What kinds of appetizers do you have?

We have stuffed mushrooms, tomato salads, and grilled onions.

Which would you rather have — steak or fish?

I'd like the New York sirloin steak, please.

STEP 1 통문장 말하기

486 제 스테이크는 웰던으로 해주세요.
완전히 익힌, 웰던으로 익힌 well-done

487 그녀와 같은 걸로 주세요.
~와 동일한 것 the same as

488 후추는 빼주세요.
(음식 주문시) 빼다 hold

489 이 나이프가 더럽네요. 깨끗한 것으로 가져다주시겠어요?
가져오다 bring

490 이제 디저트를 드실 준비가 되셨나요?
디저트, 후식 dessert   ~에 대해 준비된 ready for

STEP 2 통문장 외우기

I'd like my steak well-done.

I'll have the same as her.

Please hold the peppers.

This knife is dirty. Would you bring me a clean one, please?

Are you ready for your dessert now?

STEP 1 통문장 말하기

491 특별 후식이 있나요?

492 아이스크림 세 가지 맛 중에서 선택할 수 있어요.
맛 flavor

493 계산서를 주시겠어요?
계산서 check

494 이 식당은 지역 주민들에게 매우 인기 있는 것 같네요.
지역의 local ~처럼 보이다 seem to

495 그들은 이 식당에서 아주 훌륭한 음식을 제공해요.
(음식을) 제공하다 serve

STEP 2 통문장 외우기

Do you have any special desserts?

You have your choice of 3 flavors of ice cream.

May I have the check, please?

This restaurant seems to be very popular with local people.

They serve very good food in this restaurant.

STEP 3 패턴으로 훈련하기

❶ What kinds of | appetizers / salad / beverages* | do you have?

*음료

❷ Which would you rather have — | steak / fried chicken / ribs* | or fish?

*갈비

❸ I'd like | the New York sirloin steak / the tenderloin* steak / vegetable soup |, please.

*안심

❹ I'd like my steak | well-done / rare* / medium / medium rare / medium well-done |.

*살짝 익힌

❺ I'll have | the same as her / the usual* / mashed* potatoes and green beans |.

*늘 먹던 음식
*으깬

❻ Please hold the | peppers |.
               | onions |
               | mayonnaise* |

*마요네즈

❼ Are you ready for your | dessert | now?
                        | main course |
                        | coffee |

❽ You have your choice of 3 | flavors | of | ice cream |.
                            | kinds | | salad dressing |
                            | varieties* | | fresh fruit |

*다양함, 여러 종류

❾ May I have | the check |, please?
             | another cup of coffee |
             | a glass of water |

❿ This restaurant seems to be | very popular with local people |.
                              | busy all the time |
                              | quite clean and new |

STEP 4 대화로 훈련하기

A ❶ 주문하시겠어요?
B We'll start off with some appetizers.

A ❷ 어떤 종류의 애피타이저가 있나요?
B We have stuffed mushrooms, tomato salads, and grilled onions.

A ❸ 스테이크와 생선 요리 중에 어느 것을 드시겠어요?
B I'll have the steak, please.

A How would you like your steak done?
B ❹ 제 스테이크는 웰던으로 해주세요.

A I'd like the New York sirloin steak, please.
B ❺ 그녀와 같은 걸로 주세요.

A How spicy would you like that?
B Not too spicy and ❻ 후추는 빼주세요.

A **⑦ 이 나이프가 더럽네요. 깨끗한 것으로 가져다주시겠어요?**

B I'm sorry, ma'am. We'll bring a new one right over.

A Do you have any special desserts?

B **⑧ 아이스크림 세 가지 맛 중에서 선택할 수 있어요.**

A **⑨ 계산서를 주시겠어요?**

B I'll be right back with that, sir.

A **⑩ 이 식당은 지역 주민들에게 매우 인기 있는 것 같네요.**

B The service here is excellent in this restaurant.

ANSWERS!!

1 May I take your order?   2 What kinds of appetizers do you have?
3 Which would you rather have — steak or fish?   4 I'd like my steak well-done.
5 I'll have the same as her.   6 please hold the peppers.
7 This knife is dirty. Would you bring me a clean one, please?
8 You have your choice of 3 flavors of ice cream.   9 May I have the check, please?
10 This restaurant seems to be very popular with local people.

34 영화 및 공연 관람

STEP 1 통문장 말하기

496 오늘 밤에 영화를 보러 갑시다.
영화를 보다 see a movie

497 영화 상영 시간이 얼마나 돼요?
(특정 시간 동안) 지속되다 last

498 9시에 시작해서 11시 30분에 끝나요.
끝나다 end

499 낭만적인 줄거리예요.

500 지금까지 나온 로맨스물 중 최고래요.
지금까지, 일찍이 ever

STEP 2 통문장 외우기

Let's go see a movie tonight.

How long does the movie last?

It starts at 9 and ends at 11:30.

It's a romantic story.

They say it's the best romance movie ever.

STEP 1　통문장 말하기

501　저는 로맨스물보다 공상 과학물이 더 좋아요.
　　　　　　　　　　　공상 과학물 sci-fi[science fiction]

502　<스타워즈> 입장권 2장 주세요.

503　죄송합니다, 고객님. 그 영화는 매진됐습니다.
　　　　　　　　　　　　　　　다 팔린, 매진된 sold out

504　저는 어젯밤에 친구들과 공연을 보러 나갔어요.

505　붙어 있는 세 자리를 샀어요.
　　　　　　　　　자리, 좌석 seat

STEP 2 통문장 외우기

I like sci-fi better than romance.

2 tickets for *Star Wars*, please.

I'm sorry, ma'am. The movie is sold out.

I went out to see a show with my friends last night.

I got us three seats together.

STEP 1 통문장 말하기

506 우리가 그곳에 도착했을 때 연극은 이미 시작됐어요.
~할 무렵에 by the time

507 극장 안내원이 우리를 좌석까지 안내해줬어요.
좌석 안내원 usher 　　　　　　　　　　안내하다 show

508 연극 출연진에 유명한 배우도 있었어요.
포함하다 include

509 그 공연에서 그는 정말 훌륭했어요.
(믿을 수 없을 정도로) 훌륭한 incredible

510 그 공연은 좋았고 모두 즐거워했어요.

STEP 2 통문장 외우기

By the time we got there, the play had already begun.

The usher showed us to our seats.

The cast of the play included a famous actor.

He was incredible in the show.

The show was good and everybody enjoyed it.

STEP 3 패턴으로 훈련하기

❶ How long does the | movie / show / play* | last?   *연극

❷ It | starts / begins / goes on | at 9 and | ends / finishes / is over* | at 11:30.   *끝나다

❸ They say it's the best | romance / action / thriller* | movie ever.   *스릴러물

❹ I like | sci-fi / fantasy / horror* | better than romance.   *공포물

❺ I'm sorry, ma'am. The movie is | sold out / over / canceled* .   *취소된

⑥ I went out to see a show / see a musical* / watch a movie with my friends.

*뮤지컬

⑦ By the time we got there, the play / first act / second scene* had already begun.

*(연극, 오페라의) 장(場)

⑧ The usher / staff / attendant* / guide showed us to our seats.

*안내원

⑨ The cast of the play included a famous actor / actress / opera singer / Hollywood star .

⑩ The show was good / funny / quite amusing* / very entertaining* and everybody enjoyed it.

*재미있는, 즐거운
*즐거움을 주는

STEP 4 대화로 훈련하기

A ① **오늘 밤에 영화를 보러 갑시다.**
B Great idea. What would you like to watch?

A ② **영화 상영 시간이 얼마나 돼요?**
B It starts at 9 and ends at 11:30.

A What kind of movie is it?
B ③ **낭만적인 줄거리예요.**

A ④ **지금까지 나온 로맨스물 중 최고래요.**
B Still, I like sci-fi better than romance.

A 2 tickets for *Star Wars*, please.
B ⑤ **죄송합니다, 고객님. 그 영화는 매진됐습니다.**

A Where were you last night?
B ⑥ **저는 어젯밤에 친구들과 공연을 보러 나갔어요.**

A Did you buy the tickets?
B Sure, ❼ 붙어 있는 세 자리를 샀어요.

A Were you able to make the play on time?
B ❽ 우리가 그곳에 도착했을 때 연극은 이미 시작됐어요.

A Did you find your seats in the theater?
B ❾ 극장 안내원이 우리를 좌석까지 안내해줬어요.

A ❿ 그 공연은 좋았고 모두 즐거워했어요.
B I know! The actors were also incredible.

ANSWERS!!

1 Let's go see a movie tonight.   2 How long does the movie last?   3 It's a romantic story.
4 They say it's the best romance movie ever.   5 I'm sorry, ma'am. The movie is sold out.
6 I went out to see a show with my friends last night.   7 I got us three seats together.
8 By the time we got there, the play had already begun.
9 The usher showed us to our seats.   10 The show was good and everybody enjoyed it.

DAY 35 예약

STEP 1 통문장 말하기

511 예약이 가능한 자리가 있어요?

512 7시에 5명 자리를 예약하고 싶어요.

513 7시 대신에 8시는 어떠세요?
~대신에 instead of

514 예약을 확인하고 싶은데요.
예약 reservation

515 15분 정도 늦을 것 같아요. 괜찮나요?
늦어지다 run late

STEP 2 통문장 외우기

Do you have any tables available?

I'd like a table for 5 at 7.

How about 8 o'clock instead of 7?

I'd like to confirm my reservation.

We're running about 15 minutes late. Is that all right?

STEP 1 통문장 말하기

516 예약을 취소하려고 전화했어요.
취소하다 cancel

517 그레이 선생님과 진료 예약을 하고 싶어요.
만날 약속[예약]을 하다 make an appointment

518 고객님의 예약은 다음주 목요일 10시가 될 겁니다.

519 저는 목요일 빼고 아무 요일이나 올 수 있어요.
~을 제외하고는 except

520 약속을 월요일에서 수요일로 바꾸고 싶어요.
A에서 B로 from A to B

STEP 2 통문장 외우기

I'm calling to cancel a reservation.

I'd like to make an appointment to see Dr. Grey.

Your appointment will be next Thursday at 10 o'clock.

I can come any day except Thursday.

I'd like to change my appointment from Monday to Wednesday.

STEP 1 통문장 말하기

521 바빠서 예약을 못 지켰어요.

522 예약을 취소하겠다고 병원에 전화하지 못했네요.
~하지 못하다 fail to

523 오늘 전기 기사에게 와 달라고 전화할게요.
전기 기사 electrician

524 오늘 예약이 비어 있는 시간 있어요?
빈자리 opening

525 오기 전에 전화 주세요. 그렇지 않으면 저희가 집에 없을 수도 있어요.
~하지 않을 수 있다 might not

STEP 2 통문장 외우기

I couldn't keep my appointment because I was busy.

I failed to call the hospital to cancel my appointment.

I'm going to call an electrician to come today.

Do you have any openings today?

Please call before you come. Otherwise, we might not be home.

STEP 3 패턴으로 훈련하기

❶ Do you have any [tables / rooms / cars] available?

❷ I'd like a table [for 5 / by the window / in a non-smoking* area] at 7.   *금연

❸ I'd like to [make / have / get / arrange*] an appointment to see Dr. Grey.   *마련하다, 잡다

❹ I'm calling to [cancel / confirm* / change] a reservation.   *확인하다

❺ I can come any day [except / but* / other than*] Thursday.   *~ 외에   *~ 외에

⑥ I'd like to change my appointment from

Monday	to	Wednesday
9 a.m.		11 a.m
July 28		July 31

⑦ I couldn't keep / wasn't able to keep / had to postpone* / had to cancel — my appointment because I was busy.

*연기하다

⑧ I failed / forgot / neglected* — to call the hospital to cancel my appointment.

*등한시하다

⑨ I'm going to call an electrician / a plumbing technician* / a heating technician* — to come today.

*배관 기술자
*난방[보일러] 기술자

⑩ Please call before you come. Otherwise, we might not be home / be away / go out.

STEP 4 대화로 훈련하기

A ① 예약이 가능한 자리가 있어요?
B It looks like we have only 2 tables available for tonight.

A ② 7시에 5명 자리를 예약하고 싶어요.
B How about 8 o'clock instead of 7?

A Hello, this is King's. How may I help you?
B ③ 예약을 확인하고 싶은데요.

A ④ 예약을 취소하려고 전화했어요.
B Your name and phone number, please.

A ⑤ 그레이 선생님과 진료 예약을 하고 싶어요.
B When would you like to visit?

A Your appointment will be next Thursday at 10 o'clock.
B ⑥ 저는 목요일 빼고 아무 요일이나 올 수 있어요.

A **⑦ 약속을 월요일에서 수요일로 바꾸고 싶어요.**

B What time would you like?

A Next time you are unable to keep your appointment, please call us in advance.

B I'm really sorry. **⑧ 예약을 취소하겠다고 병원으로 전화하지 못했네요.**

A Oh, no! We've had another blackout.

B **⑨ 오늘 전기 기사에게 와 달라고 전화할게요.**

A **⑩ 오기 전에 전화 주세요. 그렇지 않으면 저희가 집에 없을 수도 있어요.**

B Sure, I'll call you before I leave.

ANSWERS!!

1 Do you have any tables available? 2 I'd like a table for 5 at 7.
3 I'd like to confirm my reservation. 4 I'm calling to cancel a reservation.
5 I'd like to make an appointment to see Dr. Grey. 6 I can come any day except Thursday.
7 I'd like to change my appointment from Monday to Wednesday.
8 I failed to call the hospital to cancel my appointment.
9 I'm going to call an electrician to come today.
10 Please call before you come. Otherwise, we might not be home.

36 진료

STEP 1 통문장 말하기

526 창백해 보이네요.
창백한 pale

527 의사에게 가서 진찰을 받는 게 좋겠어요.

528 뭐가 문제인가요?
문제 matter

529 어지러워요.
어지러운 dizzy

530 두통이 심해요.
심한 두통 bad headache

STEP 2 통문장 외우기

You look pale.

You'd better go see a doctor.

What's the matter?

I feel dizzy.

I have a bad headache.

STEP 1 통문장 말하기

531 오늘 몸은 좀 어때요?

532 오늘 아침은 별로 좋지 않네요.

533 어제는 아팠는데 오늘은 나아졌어요.
    아픈, 병든 sick

534 열은 없는데 아직도 기침이 나요.
    열 fever   기침 cough

535 어느 쪽 팔이 쑤셔요?
    (근육을 많이 써서) 아픈 sore

STEP 2 통문장 외우기

How are you feeling today?

I don't feel very well this morning.

I was sick yesterday, but I'm better today.

My fever is gone, but I still have a cough.

Which of your arms is sore?

STEP 1   통문장 말하기

536   오른팔이 아파요. 바로 여기가 아파요.
아프다 hurt

537   오른손이 부었네요. 아픈가요?
부어오른 swollen

538   어느 쪽 발이 아프세요? 왼쪽 발인가요?

539   다리는 어쩌다 부러졌나요?

540   계단에서 미끄러져서 넘어졌어요. 다리가 부러졌어요.
계단 stair   미끄러지다 slip   넘어지다 fall down

STEP 2 통문장 외우기

My right arm hurts. It hurts right here.

Your right hand is swollen. Does it hurt?

Which foot hurts? Is it the left one?

How did you break your leg?

I slipped on the stairs and fell down. I broke my leg.

STEP 3　패턴으로 훈련하기

① You look   pale / exhausted / worried and nervous*   .

*불안한

② You'd better / You should / You ought to   go see a doctor.

③ I feel   dizzy / bloated* / nauseated*   .

*속이 거북한
*메스꺼운

④ I have a bad   headache / toothache* / stomachache*   .

*치통
*복통

⑤ My fever is gone, but I still have   a cough / a sore throat* / muscle pains*   .

*인후염
*근육통

❻ Which of your arms / hands / legs / feet is sore?

❼ My right arm / foot / ear hurts. It hurts right here.

❽ Your right hand / finger / toe is swollen. Does it hurt?

❾ How did you break your leg / arm / wrist* ?

*손목

❿ I slipped on the stairs and fell down. I broke my leg / ankle* / ribs .

*발목

STEP 4 대화로 훈련하기

A It's bleeding. ① 의사에게 가서 진찰을 받는 게 좋겠어요.
B Don't worry. It's just a small cut.

A What's the matter?
B ② 어지러워요.

A ③ 두통이 심해요.
B I'll bring you some medicine.

A How are you feeling today?
B ④ 오늘 아침은 별로 좋지 않네요.

A ⑤ 어제는 아팠는데 오늘은 나아졌어요.
B It looks like the treatment is working.

A ⑥ 열은 없는데 아직도 기침이 나요.
B We may need to try something else.

A Which of your arms is sore?

B ⑦ 오른팔이 아파요. 바로 여기가 아파요.

A ⑧ 오른손이 부었네요. 아픈가요?

B Yes, my fingers hurt.

A ⑨ 어느 쪽 발이 아프세요? 왼쪽 발인가요?

B Actually, I have a pain in both feet.

A How did you break your leg?

B ⑩ 계단에서 미끄러져서 넘어졌어요. 다리가 부러졌어요.

ANSWERS!!

1 You'd better go see a doctor.   2 I feel dizzy.   3 I have a bad headache.
4 I don't feel very well this morning.   5 I was sick yesterday, but I'm better today.
6 My fever is gone, but I still have a cough.   7 My right arm hurts. It hurts right here.
8 Your right hand is swollen. Does it hurt?   9 Which foot hurts? Is it the left one?
10 I slipped on the stairs and fell down. I broke my leg.

DAY 37 집 구하기

STEP 1 통문장 말하기

541 우리는 1년간 임대할 집을 알아보고 있어요.
　　　　임대하다 rent

542 이 단독 주택이 임대물로 나왔어요. 가격이 아주 싸죠.
　　　　단독 주택 single-family house　임대물로 for rent　　　　싼 물건 bargain

543 저 집은 매물로 나왔어요. 중앙난방을 갖추었죠.
　　　　매물로 for sale　　　　중앙난방 central heating

544 가구가 구비된 집을 구하세요?
　　　　가구가 구비된 furnished

545 몇 가지 주방 용품과 식탁 세트는 있어요.
　　　　품목 item

STEP 2　통문장 외우기

We are looking for a house to rent for a year.

This single-family house is for rent. It's a bargain.

That house is for sale. It has central heating.

Are you looking for a furnished house?

We have a few kitchen items and a dining room set.

STEP 1　통문장 말하기

546　우린 침실에 놓을 침대와 서랍장을 마련해야 해요.
　　　　　　　　　　서랍장 dresser

547　거실에 걸 기다란 커튼은 있는데 부엌에 걸 커튼이 필요해요.
　　　　　　　기다란 커튼 drape

548　평면도가 재미있네요. 이 집을 보여주세요.
　　　　평면도 floor plan

549　천장에서 물이 새고 현관문은 수리해야 해요.
　　　　천장 ceiling　　　　새다 leak

550　문에 잠금장치가 있나요?
　　　　　　　잠금장치, 자물쇠 lock

STEP 2 통문장 외우기

We've got to get a bed and a dresser for the bedroom.

We have drapes for the living room, but we need kitchen curtains.

This is an interesting floor plan. Please show me the house.

The ceiling leaks, and the front door needs to be fixed.

Does the door have a lock on it?

STEP 1　통문장 말하기

551　이 스위치가 고장 난 것 같아요.
(기계 등이) 작동하다 work

552　바닥재가 썩 마음에 들지 않아요. 교체해야겠어요.
재료, 소재 material　　　교체하다 replace

553　집을 페이트칠해야겠어요. 상태가 안 좋네요.
상태가 좋지 않은 in bad condition

554　그렇지만 근처에 대중교통이 있어요.
그렇지만 yet　　　대중교통 public transportation

555　가정을 꾸리기에 좋은 곳이에요.
가정을 꾸리다 raise a family

STEP 2　통문장 외우기

I don't think this switch is working.

I'm not too happy with the floor material. I need to replace it.

The house needs painting. It's in bad condition.

Yet it's near public transportation.

It's a good place to raise a family.

STEP 3　패턴으로 훈련하기

❶ We are looking for   a house / an apartment / a 2-bedroom apartment   to rent for a year.

❷ This   single-family house / townhouse* / apartment   is for rent. It's a bargain.

*연립 주택

❸ That house is for sale. It has   central heating / a backyard* / air conditioning* .

*뒷마당
*에어컨

❹ Are you looking for   a furnished / an unfurnished / a 3-bedroom   house?

❺ We've got to get   a bed and a dresser / a sofa and a table / a sink and a stove*   for the   bedroom / living room / kitchen .

*난로

❻ This is an interesting floor plan. Please show me the house / bathroom / study* .

*서재

❼ The ceiling leaks, and the front door needs to be fixed / house needs to be painted / door lock needs to be repaired .

❽ I don't think this switch / air conditioner / vacuum cleaner* is working.

*진공청소기

❾ I'm not too happy with the floor material / hot-water heater / bathtub* .

*욕조

❿ The house needs painting / repairing / remodeling* . It's in bad condition.

*개조하다

183

STEP 4 대화로 훈련하기

A **우리는 1년간 임대할 집을 알아보고 있어요.**

B This single-family house is for rent. It's a bargain.

A **저 집은 매물로 나왔어요. 중앙난방을 갖추었죠.**

B Does it have a backyard, as well?

A **가구가 구비된 집을 구하세요?**

B Yes, we'd like a fully furnished house.

A Do you need bedroom furniture?

B Yes, **우린 침실에 놓을 침대와 서랍장을 마련해야 해요.**

A **평면도가 재미있네요. 이 집을 보여주세요.**

B Come this way. I'll let you check out the house.

A It looks like this house needs to be repaired.

B You're right. **천장에서 물이 새고 현관문은 수리해야 해요.**

A ❼ 이 스위치가 고장 난 것 같아요.

B I guess the switch is OK. But the light bulbs seem to burn out quickly.

A Do you like this house?

B Sort of, but ❽ 바닥재가 썩 마음에 들지 않아요. 교체해야겠어요.

A ❾ 집을 페인트칠해야겠어요. 상태가 안 좋네요.

B Yet it's near public transportation.

A This house is in a good neighborhood.

B I agree. ❿ 가정을 꾸리기에 좋은 곳이에요.

ANSWERS!!

1 We are looking for a house to rent for a year.
2 That house is for sale. It has central heating.   3 Are you looking for a furnished house?
4 we've got to get a bed and a dresser for the bedroom.
5 This is an interesting floor plan. Please show me the house.
6 The ceiling leaks, and the front door needs to be fixed.
7 I don't think this switch is working.
8 I'm not too happy with the floor material. I need to replace it.
9 The house needs painting. It's in bad condition.   10 It's a good place to raise a family.

38 계획

STEP 1 통문장 말하기

556 내일은 뭐 할 계획이에요?
~할 계획이다 plan to

557 내일 특별한 일을 할 것 같지 않아요.
확신하지 못하다 doubt

558 내일은 휴일이라 할 일이 없어요.
휴일, 휴가 holiday

559 남자친구는 내일 뭘 계획하고 있나요?

560 그는 뭘 할지 결정 못해요.
결정하다 decide

STEP 2 통문장 외우기

What do you plan to do tomorrow?

I doubt that I'll do anything special tomorrow.

There's nothing to do because tomorrow is a holiday.

What's your boyfriend planning to do tomorrow?

He can't decide what to do.

STEP 1 통문장 말하기

561 우리는 주말 계획을 세우는 중이에요.

562 외출하는 대신 일해야 할 것 같아요.
~대신 instead of

563 산에서 며칠 보낼 수 있기를 바라고 있어요.
~하기를 바라다 hope to

564 다음 기회가 또 있다면 당신과 같이 가고 싶어요.

565 그렇다면 이번 여름에 해변으로 가는 걸 생각해볼래요?
고려하다, 깊이 생각하다 consider

STEP 2 통문장 외우기

We're trying to plan for the weekend.

I guess I'll have to work instead of going out.

I'm hoping to spend a few days in the mountains.

If there's another chance, I'd like to go with you.

Then would you consider going to the beach this summer?

STEP 1   통문장 말하기

566   당신은 원할 때 언제든 갈 수 있어요.
~할 때 언제든 whenever

567   졸업하고 뭘 할 거예요?
졸업 graduation

568   언젠가 제 회사를 차릴 거예요.
언젠가, 훗날 someday

569   아직 아무것도 계획하지 않았어요.

570   다음에 뭘 해야 할지 확신이 없어요.
확실히 아는, 확신하는 sure

STEP 2 통문장 외우기

You can go whenever you wish.

What are you doing after graduation?

I'm going to start my own company someday.

I haven't planned anything yet.

I'm not sure what to do next.

STEP 3 패턴으로 훈련하기

① What do you [plan / intend*] to do tomorrow?

*의도하다

② I doubt that I'll [do anything / go anywhere / see anyone] special tomorrow.

③ There's [nothing to do / no place to go / no one to see] because tomorrow is a holiday.

④ [What's / Where's / When is] your boyfriend planning to [do / go / leave] tomorrow?

⑤ He can't decide [what to do / where to go / who to see / when to leave].

❻ We're trying to plan for the | weekend .
| upcoming* trip
| next 5 years

*곧 있을

❼ I guess I'll have to work instead of | going out .
| watching TV
| going to the movies

❽ I'm hoping to spend a few days | in the mountains .
| on the beach
| in Thailand

❾ Then would you consider | going to the beach | this summer?
| traveling to China
| joining* us

*함께 하다, 합류하다

❿ I'm going to | start my own company | someday.
| be a college professor
| marry her and have a family

STEP 4   대화로 훈련하기

A ① 내일은 뭐 할 계획이에요?
B There's nothing to do because tomorrow is a holiday.

A Do you have any plans for tomorrow?
B ② 내일 특별한 일을 할 것 같지 않아요.

A What's your boyfriend planning to do tomorrow?
B ③ 그는 뭘 할지 결정 못해요.

A ④ 우리는 주말 계획을 세우는 중이에요.
B What do you have planned so far?

A Let's go drink some beer tonight!
B ⑤ 외출하는 대신 일해야 할 것 같아요.

A ⑥ 산에서 며칠 보낼 수 있기를 바라고 있어요.
B Sounds good. I'd like to go with you.

A 다음 기회가 또 있다면 당신과 같이 가고 싶어요.
B Then would you consider going to the beach this summer?

A 졸업하고 뭘 할 거예요?
B I'm going to start my own company someday.

A How are you going to propose to her?
B 아직 아무것도 계획하지 않았어요.

A Are you going to look for a job, or continue studying?
B 다음에 뭘 해야 할지 확신이 없어요.

ANSWERS!!

1 What do you plan to do tomorrow? 2 I doubt that I'll do anything special tomorrow.
3 He can't decide what to do. 4 We're trying to plan for the weekend.
5 I guess I'll have to work instead of going out.
6 I'm hoping to spend a few days in the mountains.
7 If there's another chance, I'd like to go with you.
8 What are you doing after graduation?
9 I haven't planned anything yet. 10 I'm not sure what to do next.

DAY 39 이동 수단

STEP 1 통문장 말하기

571 올해 어딘가에 갈 예정인가요?

572 돈이 충분히 있다면 해외로 여행 갈 거예요.
　　　　　　　　　　해외로 abroad

573 어느 나라에 가고 싶어요?

574 멕시코로 여행 가고 싶어요.
　　　　　　여행을 하다 take a trip

575 형이 제게 그곳을 적극 추천했어요.
　　　　　　　　　추천하다, 권하다 recommend

STEP 2   통문장 외우기

Are you going to go anywhere this year?

If I have enough money, I'm going to travel abroad.

Which country would you like to go to?

I'd love to take a trip to Mexico.

My brother strongly recommended that place to me.

STEP 1 통문장 말하기

576 거기까지 가는 가장 빠른 방법이 뭔가요?
가장 빠른 the quickest

577 비행기를 타고 샌프란시스코로 가서 멕시코시티로 가는 연결편을 탈 거예요.
연결 항공편 connecting flight

578 적어도 16시간이 걸리는 비행이 될 것 같아요.

579 다 합쳐서 열흘간 여행할 거예요.
다 합쳐 altogether

580 제주도에 갈 때 여객선을 타고 갈 건가요?
(사람, 차량 등을 운반하는) 여객선 ferry

STEP 2 통문장 외우기

What's the quickest way to get there?

I'm going to fly to San Francisco and take a connecting flight to Mexico City.

I guess it's a 16-hour flight at least.

Altogether I'll be traveling for 10 days.

Are you going by ferry when you go to Jeju Island?

STEP 1 통문장 말하기

581 여객선으로 가는 것보다 비행기로 가는 게 더 빨라요.

582 부산까지 고속 열차를 탔나요?
고속의 high-speed

583 저는 예매를 못 해서 버스로 갔어요.
예매[예약]하다 book

584 내일 떠나는데 아직 여행 가방을 싸지 않았어요.
(짐을) 싸다, 꾸리다 pack

585 여행 가서 즐거운 시간을 보내길 바라요.

STEP 2 통문장 외우기

It's faster to go by plane than by ferry.

Did you take the high-speed train to Busan?

I couldn't book it, so I went by bus.

I'm leaving tomorrow, but I haven't packed my suitcases yet.

I hope you have a good time on your trip.

STEP 3 패턴으로 훈련하기

① Are you going to [go / travel / visit] anywhere this year?

② If I have enough money, I'm going to travel [abroad / overseas* / through Europe].

*해외로

③ Which [country / city / part of the world] would you like to go to?

④ I'd love to [take / make / go on] a trip to Mexico.

⑤ What's the [quickest / best / cheapest] way to get there?

❻ I guess it's a 16-hour | flight / drive / train ride | at least.

❼ Are you going by | ferry / ship / train | when you go to | Jeju Island / Japan / Busan | ?

❽ It's | faster / more comfortable / more expensive | to go by plane than by ferry.

❾ I'm leaving tomorrow, but I haven't | packed my suitcases / planned the itinerary* / booked a hotel | yet.

*여행 일정표

❿ I hope you have a | good / nice / wonderful | time on your trip.

STEP 4　대화로 훈련하기

A　**❶ 올해 어딘가에 갈 예정인가요?**

B　If I have enough money, I'm going to travel abroad.

A　**❷ 어느 나라에 가고 싶어요?**

B　I'd love to take a trip to Mexico.

A　Why would you like to go there?

B　**❸ 형이 제게 그곳을 적극 추천했어요.**

A　**❹ 거기까지 가는 가장 빠른 방법이 뭔가요?**

B　Going by plane is the quickest, but costs a lot.

A　**❺ 비행기를 타고 샌프란시스코로 가서 멕시코시티로 가는 연결편을 탈 거예요.**

B　I guess it's a 16-hour flight at least.

A　How long will you be traveling there?

B　**❻ 다 합쳐서 열흘간 여행할 거예요.**

A ⑦ 제주도에 갈 때 여객선을 타고 갈 건가요?

B No, I'm afraid I'll get seasick.

A Which is faster—by plane or by ferry?

B ⑧ 여객선으로 가는 것보다 비행기로 가는 게 더 빨라요.

A Did you take the high-speed train to Busan?

B ⑨ 저는 예매를 못 해서 버스로 갔어요.

A ⑩ 내일 떠나는데 아직 여행 가방을 싸지 않았어요.

B Is there anything I can help you with?

ANSWERS!!

1 Are you going to go anywhere this year?   2 Which country would you like to go to?
3 My brother strongly recommended that place to me.
4 What's the quickest way to get there?
5 I'm going to fly to San Francisco and take a connecting flight to Mexico City.
6 Altogether I'll be traveling for 10 days.
7 Are you going by ferry when you go to Jeju Island?
8 It's faster to go by plane than by ferry.   9 I couldn't book it, so I went by bus.
10 I'm leaving tomorrow, but I haven't packed my suitcases yet.

40 여행 준비

STEP 1   통문장 말하기

586 공항에서 당신을 배웅할게요.
~을 배웅하다 see ~ off

587 떠나기 전에 할 일이 많아요.

588 시간이 이렇게 빨리 지나간 줄 미처 몰랐어요.
알아차리다 realize

589 우선 은행에 들러 환전을 좀 해야 해요.
들르다 drop by   환전하다 exchange

590 몇 개월간 여행하는 데 돈이 아주 많이 들 거예요.

STEP 2 통문장 외우기

I'll see you off at the airport.

I've got a lot of things to do before I leave.

I didn't realize the time had passed so quickly.

For one thing, I've got to drop by the bank to exchange some money.

It'll cost me so much to travel for months.

STEP 1 통문장 말하기

591 방금 뭔가 기억났어요! 여권을 신청해야 해요.
~을 신청하다 apply for

592 여행사에 연락하는 걸 제게 알려줘서 다행이에요.

593 당신이 그 말을 하지 않았다면 전혀 생각조차 못 했을 거예요.
말하다, 언급하다 mention

594 인터넷 서비스 끊는 것을 하마터면 잊을 뻔했어요.
~이 끊어지게 하다 have ~ disconnected

595 지금 당신이 탈 항공편 탑승 안내를 하고 있어요. 겨우 시간에 맞출 수 있겠는데요.
간신히, 가까스로 barely

STEP 2 통문장 외우기

I just remembered something! I have to apply for a passport.

It's a good thing you reminded me to call the travel agency.

I never would have thought of it if you hadn't mentioned it.

I almost forgot to have the Internet service disconnected.

They're calling your flight now. You barely have time to make it.

STEP 1 통문장 말하기

596 뛰어야 해요, 그렇지 않으면 뒤처질 거예요.
뒤처지다 left behind

597 안전하게 도착했다는 문자를 우리에게 잊지 말고 보내줘요.
~에게 알리다 let ~ know 문자를 보내다 text

598 제가 분명 뭔가를 잊어버린 것 같은데 지금은 너무 늦었네요.
잊어버리다 forget

599 세관에 신고할 품목이 있나요?
세관에 신고하다 declare for customs

600 기내용 가방에 반드시 액체류를 넣지 않도록 하세요.
기내용 가방 carry-on   ~을 확실히 하다 make sure   액체 liquid

STEP 2 통문장 외우기

You'd better run, or you're going to be left behind.

Don't forget to text to let us know you arrived safely.

I'm sure I've forgotten something, but it's too late now.

Do you have anything to declare for customs?

Make sure you don't have any liquids in your carry-ons.

STEP 3   패턴으로 훈련하기

① I'll **see you off / drop you off* / say good-bye to you** at the airport.

*내려주다

② I've got a lot of things to **do / take care of* / deal with***.

*처리하다
*(문제, 과제 등을) 처리하다

③ I **didn't realize / didn't know / had no idea*** the time had passed so quickly.

*~에 대해 전혀 모르다

④ For one thing, I've got to drop by the bank to **exchange some money / get some money / cash* the check**.

*현금으로 바꾸다

⑤ **It's a good thing / Fortunately*, / Luckily,** you reminded me to call the travel agency.

*다행스럽게도

212

❻ I never would have thought of it | if you hadn't mentioned it.
I would have forgotten it
It would have slipped my mind*

*잊어버리다

❼ I almost forgot to have | the Internet service disconnected .
milk delivery stopped
my roaming service* activated*

*로밍 서비스 / *활성화시키다

❽ They're calling your flight now. You | barely | have time to make it.
hardly*
just

*거의 ~이 없다

❾ You'd better run, or you're going to | be left behind .
miss your flight

❿ Don't forget to | text | to let us know you arrived safely.
call
email

STEP 4 대화로 훈련하기

A: I'm leaving for Canada tomorrow.
B: ① 공항에서 당신을 배웅할게요.

A: Your departure date is coming closer.
B: ② 시간이 이렇게 빨리 지나간 줄 미처 몰랐어요.

A: Do you still have things to do before you leave?
B: ③ 우선 은행에 들러 환전을 좀 해야 해요.

A: What do you need so much money for?
B: ④ 몇 개월간 여행하는 데 돈이 아주 많이 들 거예요.

A: ⑤ 방금 뭔가 기억났어요! 여권을 신청해야 해요.
B: I hope it's not too late.

A: Did you buy travel insurance?
B: ⑥ 당신이 그 말을 하지 않았다면 전혀 생각조차 못 했을 거예요.

A   Don't forget to call the gas company before you leave.
B   ❼ 인터넷 서비스 끊는 것을 하마터면 잊을 뻔했어요.

A   They're calling my flight now. I barely have time to make it.
B   ❽ 뛰어야 해요, 그렇지 않으면 뒤처질 거예요.

A   ❾ 안전하게 도착했다는 문자를 우리에게 잊지 말고 보내줘요.
B   OK, I will. Thanks for your ride.

A   I'm sure I've forgotten something, but it's too late now.
B   ❿ 세관에 신고할 품목이 있나요?

ANSWERS!!

1 I'll see you off at the airport.   2 I didn't realize the time had passed so quickly.
3 For one thing, I've got to drop by the bank to exchange some money.
4 It'll cost me so much to travel for months.
5 I just remembered something! I have to apply for a passport.
6 I never would have thought of it if you hadn't mentioned it.
7 I almost forgot to have the Internet service disconnected.
8 You'd better run, or you're going to be left behind.
9 Don't forget to text to let us know you arrived safely.
10 Do you have anything to declare for customs?

**Ready For
The Next Book**

**Ready For
The Next Book**

I'll see you off at the airport.

I've got a lot of things to do before I leave.

I didn't realize the time had passed so quickly.

For one thing, I've got to drop by the bank to exchange some money.

It'll cost me so much to travel for months.

I just remembered something! I have to apply for a passport.

It's a good thing you reminded me to call the travel agency.

I never would have thought of it if you hadn't mentioned it.

I almost forgot to have the Internet service disconnected.

They're calling your flight now. You barely have time to make it.

You'd better run, or you're going to be left behind.

Don't forget to text to let us know you arrived safely.

I'm sure I've forgotten something, but it's too late now.

Do you have anything to declare for customs?

Make sure you don't have any liquids in your carry-ons.

DAY 40 여행 준비

586 공항에서 당신을 배웅할게요.

587 떠나기 전에 할 일이 많아요.

588 시간이 이렇게 빨리 지나간 줄 미처 몰랐어요.

589 우선 은행에 들러 환전을 좀 해야 해요.

590 몇 개월간 여행하는 데 돈이 아주 많이 들 거예요.

---

591 방금 뭐가 기억났어요! 여권을 신청해야 해요.

592 여행사에 연락하는 걸 제게 알려줘서 다행이에요.

593 당신이 그 말을 하지 않았다면 전혀 생각조차 못 했을 거예요.

594 인터넷 서비스 끊는 것을 하마터면 잊을 뻔했어요.

595 지금 당신이 탈 항공편 탑승 안내를 하고 있어요.
겨우 시간에 맞출 수 있겠는데요.

---

596 뛰어야 해요, 그렇지 않으면 뒤처질 거예요.

597 안전하게 도착했다는 문자를 우리에게 잊지 말고 보내줘요.

598 제가 분명 뭐가를 잊어버린 것 같은데 지금은 너무 늦었네요.

599 세관에 신고할 품목이 있나요?

600 기내용 가방에 반드시 액체류를 넣지 않도록 하세요.

Are you going to go anywhere this year?

If I have enough money, I'm going to travel abroad.

Which country would you like to go to?

I'd love to take a trip to Mexico.

My brother strongly recommended that place to me.

What's the quickest way to get there?

I'm going to fly to San Francisco and take a connecting flight to Mexico City.

I guess it's a 16-hour flight at least.

Altogether I'll be traveling for 10 days.

Are you going by ferry when you go to Jeju Island?

It's faster to go by plane than by ferry.

Did you take the high-speed train to Busan?

I couldn't book it, so I went by bus.

I'm leaving tomorrow, but I haven't packed my suitcases yet.

I hope you have a good time on your trip.

DAY 39 이동 수단

571 올해 어딘가에 갈 예정인가요?

572 돈이 충분히 있다면 해외로 여행 갈 거예요.

573 어느 나라에 가고 싶어요?

574 멕시코로 여행 가고 싶어요.

575 형이 제게 그곳을 적극 추천했어요.

---

576 거기까지 가는 가장 빠른 방법이 뭔가요?

577 비행기를 타고 샌프란시스코로 가서 멕시코시티로 가는 연결편을 탈 거예요.

578 적어도 16시간이 걸리는 비행이 될 것 같아요.

579 다 합쳐서 열흘간 여행할 거예요.

580 제주도에 갈 때 여객선을 타고 갈 건가요?

---

581 여객선으로 가는 것보다 비행기로 가는 게 더 빨라요.

582 부산까지 고속 열차를 탔나요?

583 저는 예매를 못 해서 버스로 갔어요.

584 내일 떠나는데 아직 여행 가방을 싸지 않았어요.

585 여행 가서 즐거운 시간을 보내길 바라요.

What do you plan to do tomorrow?

I doubt that I'll do anything special tomorrow.

There's nothing to do because tomorrow is a holiday.

What's your boyfriend planning to do tomorrow?

He can't decide what to do.

We're trying to plan for the weekend.

I guess I'll have to work instead of going out.

I'm hoping to spend a few days in the mountains.

If there's another chance, I'd like to go with you.

Then would you consider going to the beach this summer?

You can go whenever you wish.

What are you doing after graduation?

I'm going to start my own company someday.

I haven't planned anything yet.

I'm not sure what to do next.

DAY 38 계획

556 내일은 뭐 할 계획이에요?

557 내일 특별한 일을 할 것 같지 않아요.

558 내일은 휴일이라 할 일이 없어요.

559 남자친구는 내일 뭘 계획하고 있나요?

560 그는 뭘 할지 결정 못해요.

---

561 우리는 주말 계획을 세우는 중이에요.

562 외출하는 대신 일해야 할 것 같아요.

563 산에서 며칠 보낼 수 있기를 바라고 있어요.

564 다음 기회가 또 있다면 당신과 같이 가고 싶어요.

565 그렇다면 이번 여름에 해변으로 가는 걸 생각해볼래요?

---

566 당신은 원할 때 언제든 갈 수 있어요.

567 졸업하고 뭘 할 거예요?

568 언젠가 제 회사를 차릴 거예요.

569 아직 아무것도 계획하지 않았어요.

570 다음에 뭘 해야 할지 확신이 없어요.

We are looking for a house to rent for a year.

This single-family house is for rent. It's a bargain.

That house is for sale. It has central heating.

Are you looking for a furnished house?

We have a few kitchen items and a dining room set.

We've got to get a bed and a dresser for the bedroom.

We have drapes for the living room, but we need kitchen curtains.

This is an interesting floor plan. Please show me the house.

The ceiling leaks, and the front door needs to be fixed.

Does the door have a lock on it?

I don't think this switch is working.

I'm not too happy with the floor material. I need to replace it.

The house needs painting. It's in bad condition.

Yet it's near public transportation.

It's a good place to raise a family.

DAY 37 집 구하기

541 우리는 1년간 임대할 집을 알아보고 있어요.

542 이 단독 주택이 임대물로 나왔어요. 가격이 아주 싸죠.

543 저 집은 매물로 나왔어요. 중앙난방을 갖추었죠.

544 가구가 구비된 집을 구하세요?

545 몇 가지 주방 용품과 식탁 세트는 있어요.

---

546 우린 침실에 놓을 침대와 서랍장을 마련해야 해요.

547 거실에 걸 기다란 커튼은 있는데 부엌에 걸 커튼이 필요해요.

548 평면도가 재미있네요. 이 집을 보여주세요.

549 천장에서 물이 새고 현관문은 수리해야 해요.

550 문에 잠금장치가 있나요?

---

551 이 스위치가 고장 난 것 같아요.

552 바닥재가 썩 마음에 들지 않아요. 교체해야겠어요.

553 집을 페인트칠해야겠어요. 상태가 안 좋네요.

554 그렇지만 근처에 대중교통이 있어요.

555 가정을 꾸리기에 좋은 곳이에요.

You look pale.

You'd better go see a doctor.

What's the matter?

I feel dizzy.

I have a bad headache.

How are you feeling today?

I don't feel very well this morning.

I was sick yesterday, but I'm better today.

My fever is gone, but I still have a cough.

Which of your arms is sore?

My right arm hurts. It hurts right here.

Your right hand is swollen. Does it hurt?

Which foot hurts? Is it the left one?

How did you break your leg?

I slipped on the stairs and fell down. I broke my leg.

DAY 36 진료

526 창백해 보이네요.

527 의사에게 가서 진찰을 받는 게 좋겠어요.

528 뭐가 문제인가요?

529 어지러워요.

530 두통이 심해요.

---

531 오늘 몸은 좀 어때요?

532 오늘 아침은 별로 좋지 않네요.

533 어제는 아팠는데 오늘은 나아졌어요.

534 열은 없는데 아직도 기침이 나요.

535 어느 쪽 팔이 쑤셔요?

---

536 오른팔이 아파요. 바로 여기가 아파요.

537 오른손이 부었네요. 아픈가요?

538 어느 쪽 발이 아프세요? 왼쪽 발인가요?

539 다리는 어쩌다 부러졌나요?

540 계단에서 미끄러져서 넘어졌어요. 다리가 부러졌어요.

Do you have any tables available?

I'd like a table for 5 at 7.

How about 8 o'clock instead of 7?

I'd like to confirm my reservation.

We're running about 15 minutes late. Is that all right?

I'm calling to cancel a reservation.

I'd like to make an appointment to see Dr. Grey.

Your appointment will be next Thursday at 10 o'clock.

I can come any day except Thursday.

I'd like to change my appointment from Monday to Wednesday.

I couldn't keep my appointment because I was busy.

I failed to call the hospital to cancel my appointment.

I'm going to call an electrician to come today.

Do you have any openings today?

Please call before you come. Otherwise, we might not be home.

35 예약

511 예약이 가능한 자리가 있어요?

512 7시에 5명 자리를 예약하고 싶어요.

513 7시 대신에 8시는 어떠세요?

514 예약을 확인하고 싶은데요.

515 15분 정도 늦을 것 같아요. 괜찮나요?

516 예약을 취소하려고 전화했어요.

517 그레이 선생님과 진료 예약을 하고 싶어요.

518 고객님의 예약은 다음주 목요일 10시가 될 겁니다.

519 저는 목요일 빼고 아무 요일이나 올 수 있어요.

520 약속을 월요일에서 수요일로 바꾸고 싶어요.

521 바빠서 예약을 못 지켰어요.

522 예약을 취소하겠다고 병원에 전화하지 못했네요.

523 오늘 전기 기사에게 와 달라고 전화할게요.

524 오늘 예약이 비어 있는 시간 있어요?

525 오기 전에 전화 주세요. 그렇지 않으면 저희가 집에 없을 수도 있어요.

Let's go see a movie tonight.

How long does the movie last?

It starts at 9 and ends at 11:30.

It's a romantic story.

They say it's the best romance movie ever.

I like sci-fi better than romance.

2 tickets for *Star Wars*, please.

I'm sorry, ma'am. The movie is sold out.

I went out to see a show with my friends last night.

I got us three seats together.

By the time we got there, the play had already begun.

The usher showed us to our seats.

The cast of the play included a famous actor.

He was incredible in the show.

The show was good and everybody enjoyed it.

34 영화 및 공연 관람

496 오늘 밤에 영화를 보러 갑시다.

497 영화 상영 시간이 얼마나 돼요?

498 9시에 시작해서 11시 30분에 끝나요.

499 낭만적인 줄거리예요.

500 지금까지 나온 로맨스물 중 최고래요.

501 저는 로맨스물보다 공상 과학물이 더 좋아요.

502 <스타워즈> 입장권 2장 주세요.

503 죄송합니다, 고객님. 그 영화는 매진됐습니다.

504 저는 어젯밤에 친구들과 공연을 보러 나갔어요.

505 붙어 있는 세 자리를 샀어요.

506 우리가 그곳에 도착했을 때 연극은 이미 시작됐어요.

507 극장 안내원이 우리를 좌석까지 안내해줬어요.

508 연극 출연진에 유명한 배우도 있었어요.

509 그 공연에서 그는 정말 훌륭했어요.

510 그 공연은 좋았고 모두 즐거워했어요.

May I take your order?

What kinds of appetizers do you have?

We have stuffed mushrooms, tomato salads, and grilled onions.

Which would you rather have — steak or fish?

I'd like the New York sirloin steak, please.

I'd like my steak well-done.

I'll have the same as her.

Please hold the peppers.

This knife is dirty. Would you bring me a clean one, please?

Are you ready for your dessert now?

Do you have any special desserts?

You have your choice of 3 flavors of ice cream.

May I have the check, please?

This restaurant seems to be very popular with local people.

They serve very good food in this restaurant.

DAY 33 음식 주문

481 주문하시겠어요?

482 어떤 종류의 애피타이저가 있나요?

483 속을 채운 버섯, 토마토 샐러드, 그리고 그릴에 구운 양파가 있습니다.

484 스테이크와 생선 요리 중에 어느 것을 드시겠어요?

485 뉴욕 등심 스테이크로 주세요.

---

486 제 스테이크는 웰던으로 해주세요.

487 그녀와 같은 걸로 주세요.

488 후추는 빼주세요.

489 이 나이프가 더럽네요. 깨끗한 것으로 가져다주시겠어요?

490 이제 디저트를 드실 준비가 되셨나요?

---

491 특별 후식이 있나요?

492 아이스크림 세 가지 맛 중에서 선택할 수 있어요.

493 계산서를 주시겠어요?

494 이 식당은 지역 주민들에게 매우 인기 있는 것 같네요.

495 그들은 이 식당에서 아주 훌륭한 음식을 제공해요.

I bought this on Amazon.

What forms of payment do they accept?

You can only pay by credit card or PayPal.

Is it cheaper than buying at the department store?

Of course, I got this bag at today's special price.

What if I'm not satisfied with the product?

They have 30 day money-back guarantee.

Do they ship to Korea?

How much is it to get items delivered to Seoul?

The shipping charge will depend on the size and weight of your order.

How long will it take to arrive?

Can it be shipped overnight?

No, I think it'll take 4 to 5 days at least.

Can I track the shipment online?

Can I change the delivery address?

DAY 32 온라인 쇼핑

466 이거 아마존에서 샀어요.

467 어떤 결제 방식이 가능한가요?

468 신용카드나 페이팔로만 지불할 수 있어요.

469 백화점에서 사는 것보다 저렴한가요?

470 물론이죠, 이 가방은 오늘의 특가로 샀는걸요.

---

471 만약 제가 제품에 만족하지 못하면 어쩌죠?

472 30일 환불 보장 제도가 있어요.

473 한국으로 배송하나요?

474 서울까지 물건을 배달 받으려면 얼마나 들어요?

475 배송료는 주문한 물건의 크기와 무게에 따라 결정될 거예요.

---

476 도착하는 데 얼마나 걸릴까요?

477 주문한 다음 날에 배송 받을 수 있나요?

478 아니오, 최소한 4-5일은 걸릴 것 같아요.

479 배송 상황을 온라인으로 확인할 수 있나요?

480 배송 주소를 변경할 수 있나요?

I'm going shopping because I need to buy some clothes.

Can I help you with anything?

I'm just looking around.

This dress is made of silk, isn't it?

I'd like to try on this sweater.

What size would you like?

I need this in a medium.

That looks very good on you.

I love it! I'll take two.

How much is this shirt?

Is this chair on sale today?

That's a nice tablet PC, but it costs too much.

If this doesn't work, may I bring it back later?

How would you like to pay for this?

Do you take credit cards?

DAY 31 매장 쇼핑

451 옷을 좀 사야 해서 쇼핑하러 가요.

452 뭘 도와 드릴까요?

453 그냥 둘러보는 거예요.

454 이 드레스는 실크로 만들어진 거죠, 그렇지 않나요?

455 이 스웨터를 입어 보고 싶어요.

456 어떤 사이즈로 드릴까요?

457 이 옷의 중간 치수가 필요해요.

458 참 잘 어울리네요.

459 정말 좋아요! 두 벌 살게요.

460 이 셔츠는 얼마죠?

461 이 의자는 오늘 세일하나요?

462 좋은 태블릿 피시네요. 근데 너무 비싸요.

463 이게 작동되지 않으면 나중에 다시 가져와도 되나요?

464 이건 어떻게 지불하시겠어요?

465 신용카드는 받나요?

Why don't you get dressed now? You might miss the bus.

You'd better wear a heavy jacket. It's chilly today.

What are you going to wear today?

I'm going to wear my black suit.

You need to have that suit cleaned and pressed.

All my suits are dirty. I don't have anything to wear.

I have 2 suits that need to be dry-cleaned.

I have some shirts to take to the cleaners.

I've got to get these shirts washed and ironed.

This dress doesn't fit me anymore.

I can't fasten this button.

I've outgrown some of my clothes.

These shoes are worn out.

I didn't notice you were wearing your new clothes.

I came in, changed my clothes, and went out again.

DAY 30 의복 관리

436 이제 옷을 입지 않겠어요? 그러다 버스를 놓치겠어요.

437 두꺼운 재킷을 입는 게 좋을 거예요. 오늘은 쌀쌀해요.

438 오늘 뭘 입을 거예요?

439 검은색 정장을 입을 거예요.

440 그 정장을 세탁하고 다림질해야 해요.

441 제 정장이 모두 더러워요. 입을 게 없어요.

442 드라이클리닝을 해야 하는 정장이 두 벌 있어요.

443 세탁소에 가져갈 셔츠들이 좀 있어요.

444 이 셔츠들을 세탁하고 다림질해야 해요.

445 이 드레스는 더 이상 제게 맞지 않네요.

446 이 단추를 못 채우겠어요.

447 제가 너무 자라서 어떤 옷들은 안 맞아요.

448 이 구두들은 닳았어요.

449 새 옷을 입고 있는 걸 미처 몰랐어요.

450 저는 들어와서 옷을 갈아입고 다시 나갔어요.

What time are you going to get up tomorrow?

I'll probably get up at 6:30.

What will you do then?

After I get dressed, I'll have breakfast.

What will you have for breakfast tomorrow?

I guess I'll have eggs and toast for breakfast.

After breakfast, I'll get ready to go to work.

I'll leave the house at 8 o'clock and get to the office at 8:30.

I'll probably go out for lunch at about 12:30.

I'll finish working at 6 and get home by 8 o'clock.

Are you going to have dinner at home tomorrow night?

Do you think you'll go to the movies tomorrow morning?

I think I'll stay home and watch TV.

When I get sleepy, I'll probably get ready for bed.

Do you think you'll be able to get up early tomorrow morning?

DAY 29 내일 일과

421 내일 몇 시에 일어날 거예요?

422 아마 6시 30분에 일어날 거예요.

423 그런 다음 뭘 할 거예요?

424 옷을 입은 후 아침 식사를 할 거예요.

425 내일 아침 식사로 뭘 먹을 거예요?

---

426 아침 식사로 달걀과 토스트를 먹을 것 같아요.

427 아침 식사 후에 출근 준비를 할 거예요.

428 8시에 집을 나서서 사무실에는 8시 30분에 도착할 거예요.

429 저는 아마 12시 30분쯤에 점심 식사하러 나갈 거예요.

430 저는 6시에 일을 마치고 8시까지는 집에 도착할 거예요.

---

431 내일 밤 집에서 저녁 식사할 거예요?

432 내일 아침에 영화를 보러 갈 생각인가요?

433 집에 있으면서 TV를 볼 것 같은데요.

434 졸리면 아마 자러 갈 거예요.

435 내일 아침에 일찍 일어날 수 있을 것 같아요?

Did you grow up right here in this neighborhood?

I spent my childhood in California.

I lived in California until I was 10.

Then my family moved in here.

This is where I grew up until I was 17.

There have been a lot of changes here in the last 20 years.

There used to be a grocery store on the corner.

All of those houses have been built in the last 10 years.

I love everything in this neighborhood.

Everything is so convenient in this area.

Are your neighbors friendly?

We all know each other pretty well.

Who lives next door?

A young married couple moved in next door to us.

I get along well with them.

DAY 28 거주지와 이웃

406 바로 이 동네에서 자랐나요?

407 저는 캘리포니아에서 어린 시절을 보냈어요.

408 10살이 될 때까지 캘리포니아에서 살았어요.

409 그러고 나서 우리 가족은 이곳으로 이사 왔어요.

410 이곳은 제가 17살까지 자란 곳이에요.

---

411 지난 20년간 여기에서 많은 변화들이 있었어요.

412 저 모퉁이에 식료품 가게가 있었어요.

413 저 집들은 모두 지난 10년 사이에 지어졌어요.

414 저는 이 동네의 모든 것들이 정말 좋아요.

415 이 지역에선 모든 것이 매우 편리해요.

---

416 이웃들은 친절한가요?

417 우리 모두 서로를 꽤 잘 알아요.

418 옆집엔 누가 살아요?

419 젊은 부부가 우리 옆집으로 이사 왔어요.

420 저는 그들과 잘 지내요.

We're getting married!

He asked me to marry him.

I hope you can make the wedding.

How long have you been married?

We've just married.

We're on our honeymoon.

We've been married for quite a few years.

We got married in 2007.

Is your brother married?

He's not married. He's still single.

He's been divorced for over a year.

Do you have children?

I'm going to be a father.

We had a baby last month.

Our children are grown up now.

DAY 27 결혼과 가정

391 우리 결혼해요!

392 그 사람이 저와 결혼하자고 했어요.

393 결혼식에 와주셨으면 좋겠어요.

394 결혼한 지 얼마나 됐나요?

395 이제 막 결혼했어요.

396 우리는 신혼여행 중이에요.

397 우리는 결혼한 지 몇 년 됐어요.

398 우리는 2007년에 결혼했어요.

399 남동생은 결혼했나요?

400 결혼하지 않았어요. 아직 미혼이에요.

401 그는 1년 넘게 이혼한 상태예요.

402 자녀들이 있나요?

403 곧 아빠가 될 거예요.

404 우리는 지난달에 아기를 낳았어요.

405 우리 아이들은 이제 다 컸어요.

I can't access the Internet.

You need to enter a Wi-Fi password.

Put my number in your address book.

I'll send you a text when I get home.

I dropped my cell phone and the screen is cracked.

The battery won't charge.

Send your phone to the repair center.

Why didn't you answer the phone?

I'm sorry. I set my phone to silent mode.

The memory on my phone is full because of photos and videos.

Delete some of the files to make space.

I blog from my phone.

My boss friended me on Facebook.

Now, you should "like" his every status update.

He's following you on Twitter as well.

DAY 26 스마트폰과 SNS

376 인터넷 접속이 안 돼요.

377 와이파이 비밀번호를 입력해야 해요.

378 주소록에 제 번호를 저장해 놔요.

379 집에 도착하면 문자를 보낼게요.

380 휴대폰을 떨어뜨렸더니 액정에 금이 갔어요.

---

381 배터리 충전이 안 돼요.

382 전화기를 수리점으로 보내세요.

383 왜 전화를 안 받았어요?

384 미안해요. 전화기를 무음 모드로 설정해 놓았거든요.

385 제 전화기의 메모리가 사진과 동영상 때문에 꽉 찼어요.

---

386 공간이 확보되도록 파일들을 좀 지우세요.

387 저는 휴대폰으로 블로그를 해요.

388 상사가 페이스북에서 친구 신청을 했어요.

389 이제 그가 상태를 업데이트할 때마다 '좋아요'를 눌러야겠네요.

390 그가 트위터에서도 당신을 팔로우하고 있던데요.

The phone is ringing. Can you answer it, please?

Hello, Microchips Inc. This is Janet speaking.

Hello, may I speak to Maggie?

You must have dialed the wrong number.

Could you please speak louder?

Please hold for a minute.

Someone is on the line for you.

May I ask who is calling?

I'm sorry. She's not available.

Would you like to leave a message?

Would you please tell her that I called?

Would you mind calling back sometime tomorrow?

I tried to call Mr. Cooper, but the line was busy.

I dialed the right number, but nobody answered.

You can reach him on his cell phone.

DAY 25 전화

361 전화가 울려요. 좀 받아주시겠어요?

362 여보세요, 마이크로칩 사의 재닛입니다.

363 여보세요, 매기와 통화할 수 있을까요?

364 (당신은) 전화 잘못 걸었어요.

365 더 크게 말해주시겠어요?

---

366 잠깐만 기다려주세요.

367 어떤 사람이 당신을 (전화상으로) 기다리고 있어요.

368 전화 거신 분이 누군지 물어봐도 될까요?

369 미안해요. 그녀는 전화를 받을 수 없어요.

370 메모를 남기시겠어요?

---

371 그녀에게 제가 전화했다고 전해주시겠어요?

372 내일 언제 다시 전화하시면 안 될까요?

373 쿠퍼 씨에게 전화하려고 했는데 계속 통화 중이었어요.

374 맞는 번호로 걸었는데 아무도 받지 않았어요.

375 그의 휴대폰으로 연락하면 돼요.

Excuse me, can you help me find the Hilton Hotel?

It's 2 blocks straight ahead.

Can you give me directions to the Peace Park?

Turn right at the next corner.

Can you tell me where Peach Street is?

Should I go this way, or that way?

I don't know. I'm a stranger here, too.

Which way is the movie theater?

It's just around the corner.

Do you know how far it is to Washington University?

It's a long way from here.

Go that way for 2 blocks, then turn left.

Could you tell me where the nearest subway station is?

It's across the street from the Plaza Hotel.

You can't miss it.

DAY 24 길 찾기

346 실례하지만 힐튼 호텔을 찾는 것 좀 도와줄래요?

347 곧장 앞으로 두 블록만 가면 됩니다.

348 피스 공원까지 가는 길을 알려주시겠어요?

349 다음 모퉁이에서 오른쪽으로 도세요.

350 피치로(路)가 어디 있는지 알려주시겠어요?

351 이 길로 가야 하나요, 아니면 저 길로 가야 하나요?

352 모르겠어요. 저도 여기 초행이에요.

353 영화관은 어느 방향인가요?

354 모퉁이를 돌면 바로 있어요.

355 워싱턴 대학교까지 얼마나 먼지 아세요?

356 여기서부터 한참 가야 돼요.

357 저쪽 길로 두 블록 간 다음 왼쪽으로 도세요.

358 가장 가까운 지하철역이 어디 있는지 알려주시겠어요?

359 플라자 호텔에서 길 건너편에 있어요.

360 쉽게 찾을 수 있어요.

I need your help with the chores.

Are you able to help me with the laundry?

Thank you for your help.

You're welcome.

Can you help with the housework?

Would you please take out the trash?

Will you do me a favor?

Please ask John to turn on the lights.

If you have time, will you call me tomorrow?

Would you help me lift this heavy box?

Would you please tell Mr. Peterson that I'm here?

Would you mind feeding my cat for me?

Not at all. How much should I feed him?

Could you pass the screwdriver over here?

Could I have the pepper when you're done with it?

DAY 23 부탁과 요청

331 집안일에 당신 도움이 필요해요.

332 빨래 좀 도와줄 수 있어요?

333 도와줘서 고마워요.

334 천만에요.

335 집안일을 거들어줄래요?

---

336 저 쓰레기를 내다 버려주시겠어요?

337 제 부탁 좀 들어줄래요?

338 존에게 불을 켜 달라고 해주세요.

339 시간이 있으면 내일 전화 좀 줄래요?

340 이 무거운 상자를 들어 올리는 것 좀 도와주시겠어요?

---

341 피터슨 씨에게 제가 여기 있다고 전해주시겠어요?

342 저 대신 고양이에게 먹이를 주시면 안 될까요?

343 물론이죠. 먹이를 얼마나 줘야 하죠?

344 드라이버를 이쪽으로 건네주시겠어요?

345 후추를 다 썼으면 제게 주시겠어요?

What color is your cell phone?

It's light blue.

What size laptop do you have?

One of my laptops is small, and the other one is medium size.

How long is the LAN cable for the desktop?

It is only 5 meters long.

How much does that suitcase weigh?

It weighs about 5 pounds.

It's not too heavy, but I don't know the exact weight.

Is this window wider than that one?

No, this window is just as wide as that one.

I like the shape of that table.

I prefer the round one to the square one.

How does the cloth feel?

It feels very soft.

22 사물 묘사

316 당신의 휴대폰은 무슨 색이에요?

317 연한 파란색이에요.

318 어떤 크기의 노트북을 갖고 있어요?

319 제 노트북들 중 하나는 작고, 다른 하나는 중간 크기예요.

320 그 데스크톱의 랜 케이블 길이가 얼마나 돼요?

321 길이가 겨우 5미터예요.

322 저 여행 가방은 무게가 얼마나 나가요?

323 5파운드 정도 나가요.

324 너무 무거운 건 아닌데 정확한 무게는 모르겠어요.

325 이 창문이 저 창문보다 더 넓어요?

326 아니오, 이 창문은 딱 저 창문만큼 넓어요.

327 저 테이블의 모양이 마음에 들어요.

328 저는 정사각형인 것보다 둥근 것이 더 좋아요.

329 그 옷의 촉감이 어때요?

330 아주 부드러워요.

How's the weather today?

The weather is nice today.

It's sunny!

It's quite cold today.

It's raining outside.

It'll probably clear up this afternoon.

It's been cloudy all morning.

Yesterday it rained all day.

What will the weather be like tomorrow?

It's going to snow tomorrow.

It's great weather, isn't it?

The days are getting hotter.

What's the temperature outside?

It's about 30 degrees Celsius now.

There's a cool breeze this evening.

DAY 21 날씨

301 오늘은 날씨가 어때요?

302 오늘은 날씨가 좋아요.

303 화창해요!

304 오늘은 상당히 춥네요.

305 밖에 비가 와요.

306 오늘 오후에는 아마 갤 거예요.

307 아침 내내 흐렸어요.

308 어제는 하루 종일 비가 왔어요.

309 내일은 날씨가 어떨까요?

310 내일은 눈이 올 거예요.

311 날씨가 정말 좋네요, 안 그래요?

312 날이 점점 더워지고 있어요.

313 바깥 기온이 몇 도인가요?

314 현재 기온은 섭씨 30도 정도예요.

315 오늘 저녁에는 시원한 바람이 불어요.

			1st week
			2nd week
			3rd week
			4th week

150 165 180 195 210 225 240 255 270 285 300

목표 달성 체크업

각 Day에서 내가 암기한 문장 수만큼 색칠하세요.

DAY								
DAY 21								
DAY 22								
DAY 23								
DAY 24								
DAY 25								
DAY 26								
DAY 27								
DAY 28								
DAY 29								
DAY 30								
DAY 31								
DAY 32								
DAY 33								
DAY 34								
DAY 35								
DAY 36								
DAY 37								
DAY 38								
DAY 39								
DAY 40								

0　15　30　45　60　75　90　105　120

휴·대·용

통문장
암기장

휴·대·용

통문장
암기장